SCREW YOU!

Startup Business Tips to Destroy Doubt, Especially Inside You

Tips 1-20

Tim Carthon

Startup Business Infrastructure Specialist
Advocate | Speaker | Author | Educator

Copyright© 2016. Tim Carthon.
All rights reserved.

Editor: Kelli Cordova
Cover Illustrator: Mario Smith

ISBN-13: 978-1537063515
ISBN-10: 1537063510

ACKNOWLEDGEMENTS

God and my family, especially my wonderful son TJ, for whom I work so hard to keep proud of me every single day, and my absolutely beautiful Mom. Mom, you've done more for me than anyone in my life, and I truly love and thank you for that, more than you may ever understand.

My friends, closest associates, and supporters, especially:

- Bone (*KILLER book cover, man*).
- My fellow business owner E-Dub (*focus wins the race*).
- My Music Director 'Negro Spiritual' (*talented musician with unshakable support and loyalty*).
- 'TB' (*one of the few true and talented gentlemen left in the world*).
- My phenomenal, fellow Nubian intellectual 'Nique.'
- My oh-so-wonderful 'Pameezy.'
- The amazing 'Chellisa' (☺).
- 'K-Love,' the lovely.
- 'Brina Brine,' the photography Queen.
- And the ridiculously-talented 'D-Strad' (*always on beast mode*).

My partners and sponsor, especially Fiverr® (Fiverr.com), which has been a fantastic 'road dog' in the journey toward increasing inner-city entrepreneurship and the access to affordable digital services that new businesses need. It's no wonder your company has grown the way it has. Visionaries can sense success coming. Thank you for traveling with me.

Dedicated to my wonderful, beautiful friend Anjie Perkins.

She fought cancer with everything she had, and inspired me. Love and miss you, truly (1978-2015).

TABLE OF CONTENTS

SCREW YOU! Startup Business Tips 1-20

Chapter 1: *"Own, Or Get Owned"* 1

Chapter 2: *"What Is Your 'It'? Who Are Your 'They?'"* 7

    1. In what industries do you wish to primarily spend the rest of your life?... 8
    2. What need does that industry have or what void is there to fill?.... 9
    3. Is filling that need/void feasible?... 9
    4. Who is it that can benefit the most from your products and services?.. 10

Chapter 3: *"Your Unstoppable Digital Juggernaut."* 11

Chapter 4: *"8 Hours A Day Keeps Success Away."* 17

Chapter 5: *"Customer Service is <u>Not</u> Dead, Right?* 23

Chapter 6: *"Feast on Facts, Not Feelings."* 27

Chapter 7: *"Being 'Better' Over Being 'Bigger.'"* 31

Chapter 8: *"Money = Influence."* 35

Chapter 9: *"A Little Caring. A Lot of Cash."* 41

Chapter 10: *"'Employer -vs.- Employee' Thinking."* 45

Chapter 11: *"Good Help Is Hard To Keep."* 59

Chapter 12: *"Where to Set Up Your Business Tents."* 67

Chapter 13: *"Fame, Fortune, And..."* 75

Chapter 14: *"The Art of Verbiage."* 79

CONTRACTUALLY 80
- Verbal 80
- Written 81

WRITTEN CORRESPONDENCE 82
- Titles 83
- Spelling and Punctuation Errors 83
- Same Sound, Different Meaning 84
- Email 85
- Traditional Letters 86

Chapter 15: *"Your Brand of Business."* 89

Chapter 16: *"Time Flies."* 93

Chapter 17: *"Survivors -.vs.- Thrivers. Which One Are You?"* 99

Chapter 18: *"Less Employees, More Money."* 105

Chapter 19: *"More Success Breeds More 'Support.'"* 109

Chapter 20: *"Issues -vs.- Problems."* 117

Tim Carthon's *Life Motto* 124

Works Cited 125
- Chapter 1 126
- Chapter 3 126

- Chapter 4 126
- Chapter 6 126
- Chapter 7 127
- Chapter 8 127
- Chapter 12 128
- Chapter 13 129
- Chapter 14 129
- Chapter 17 129
- Chapter 20 130

About the Author 131

INTRODUCTION

One of the most difficult things one can do in life is to follow their dreams. When I started doing business back in 2001, I had no idea the level of difficulty I'd run into on this journey.

Although for a noble cause, I did not initially spend my time learning the art of business before I jumped into the entrepreneurial fray. That was the biggest mistake of my business life...

...or so I thought.

For years I traversed a course through several businesses, and, at each turn, I ran into a slew of unforeseen walls and traps for which I was, of course, unprepared.

Through pain, loss, and temporary failure, I watched as the people for whom I sacrificed and helped selflessly for years turned their backs on me when I needed their support the most.

That opened my eyes to the depths of the world's selfishness.

Turns out that the most dangerous thing I found over the years regarding the following of one's dreams was not the direct, base-jumping path to the entrepreneurial destination, but more the ones who you attempt to carry with you or who you meet along that path.

This is because the emotional scarring from their betrayal can be devastating and something extremely difficult from which to recover, if recovery is even at all possible. However…

…I was blessed.

Instead of falling into and hardening myself within the cement of despair, I decided, like Tyler Perry®, to turn my pain into someone else's gain.

Since no one can tell you how to deal with issues better than an individual who has been through those issues, this prompted me to not only create an entrepreneurial road map inside of my economic enlightenment seminars and startup business infrastructure workshops, but to also write a series of 'mental road map' books as well for people like me.

This is the first of them.

SCREW YOU! Startup Business Tips to Destroy Doubt, Especially Inside You (Tips 1-20) simultaneously starves your fears and douses doubters' doubts, all while feeding your awakening entrepreneurial warrior with a hearty, but easily digestible startup business tips breakfast.

It brings energy to your warrior and light to the unknown so that you can tell fear and doubt **'SCREW YOU!'** and never let either of them rule your life again!

"Your life was not given to you for you. It was given to you for you to be a blessing to someone else."

~ Tim Carthon

Time to tell your fears and doubts...

SCREW YOU!

Chapter 1:

"Own, Or Get Owned."

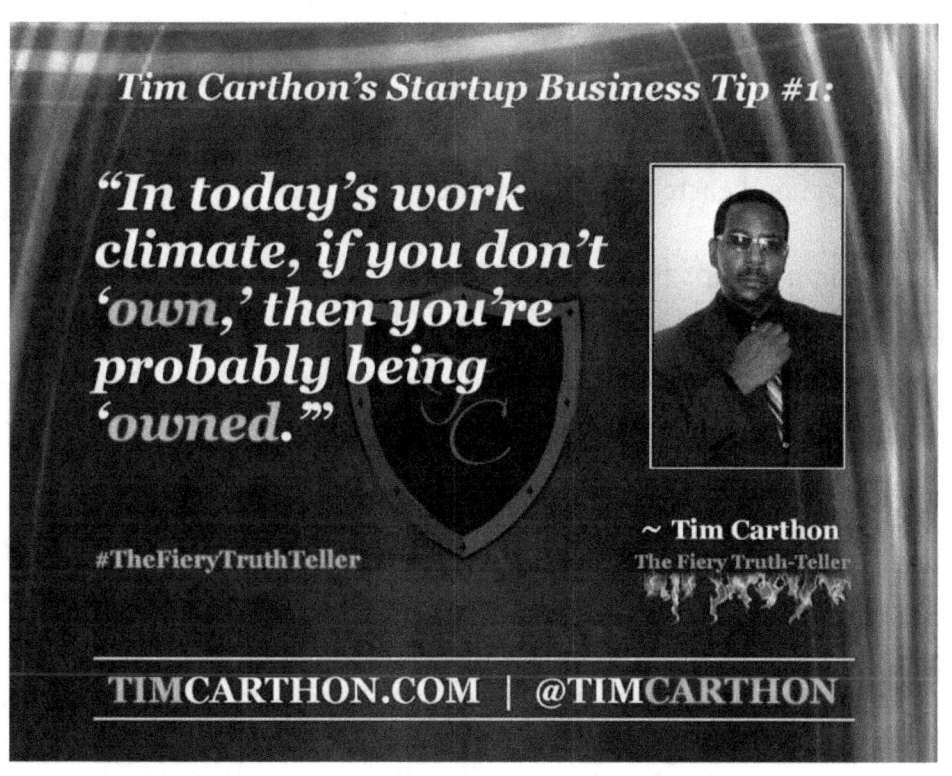

SCREW YOU! Startup Business Tips 1-20

You're laying on the beach in Maui. You're drinking that beverage that you always order. It is day 22 of your month-long stay in paradise. You look to your left and walking toward you is an absolutely amazing silhouette. It's your significant other, bringing you a platter of tropical fruits.

They lie down beside you and begin feeding you, as you gaze into each other's eyes. You savor the sweet taste of nature's nourishment and then taste the lips of the absolutely wonderful human creation God has brought to you, as the ocean waves act as the moment's soundtrack.

As your lips part and you and your significant other cuddle closely, you close your eyes and enjoy the warmth of the sun on your bodies and the warmth of the love in your hearts, as you can feel each other's beating...

...*Bump-Bump...Bump-Bump...Bump...Bump...*BEEP! *BEEP! *BEEP! *BEEP!

Your eyes open. The smile on your face evens out to nothingness, as you stare at the white ceiling above your bed and reach your hand blindly over to kill the annoying, but necessary beeping noise. You slowly sit up, wiping the sleep from your eyes as the realization of actuality sets in. You begrudgingly make your way to the shower, all to do what?

To prepare yourself physically and mentally to go to a job at a company that is owned by a person who is currently in Maui, drinking their favorite beverage, on their 22nd day of their quarterly vacation, eating tropical fruits fed to them by their

Chapter 1: Own, Or Get Owned.

significant other, as they gaze into each other's eyes and taste nature's nourishment right from each other's lips.

And that's right before they cuddle closely and enjoy the warmth of the sun on each other's bodies and the warmth of the love in their hearts they have for each other, all while they watch the sun begin to set, paid for by the company *they own* and for which *you work*.

Irony is something else, ain't it?

No one has to ask you which person you would rather be in this example (*the worker who dreams of a better life or the owner who's on a virtual constant vacation and actually lives it*). We all wish to be the owner on vacation, especially a 30-day vacation. The problem is that most people don't want to do the work it takes to reach that level of title, and there is nothing necessarily wrong with that.

Just how there have to be bosses in the world, there have to be workers in the world as well, and being a hard-working worker is an honorable thing. Unfortunately, the way that owners and their businesses tend to treat workers nowadays is far from such.

Businesses are now puppeting workers. There is no room for criticism and thereby creativity, at least not on the scale it used to be. Workers are now treated more like cattle than people. They are being forced to do overtime by companies that are now making overtime *mandatory*.

When in the world did getting extra work hours to make extra money become something that was *forced* on individuals?

Simple.

It became that when company executives realized that they could make more money by transferring the responsibility of subsidization, such as healthcare and food, to the government.

What did that do for the company executives exactly?

Transferring monetary responsibility for workers to the government made needing the workers (*in order to help generate their profits*) less necessary for companies. That, in turn, put more power into the hands of the companies, their executives, and owners.

And what could they do with that power exactly?

They could lay off more workers, make the remaining workers work harder, and get the same productivity for half the payroll costs.

Higher productivity with lower company costs. That's good, right?

No.

On top of the fact that half the workers just lost their jobs and now need to go on unemployment, subsidized by the taxpayers' government, the remaining profits the company saved from laying those workers off and cutting payroll costs is

Chapter 1: Own, Or Get Owned.

then split up not among the workers who did the productivity, but among the executives and the owners who unnecessarily forced them to work two-times harder.

See for yourself:

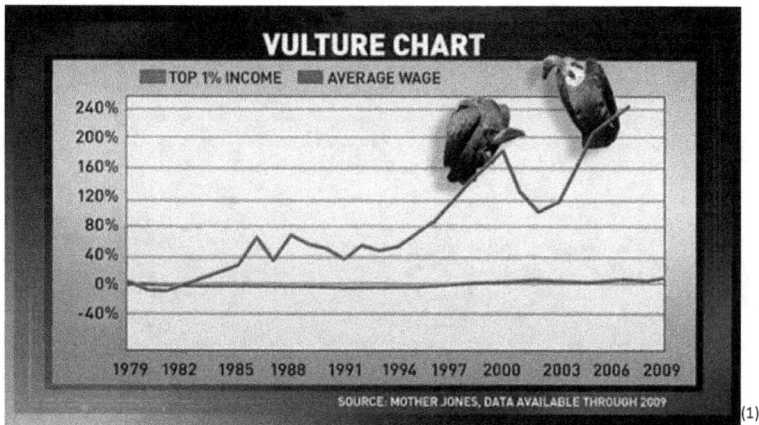
(1)

Vulture Chart Translation: Your hard work = their profit.

If you are on the ownership side of this equation, you are sitting in an amazing position; a position that allows you to live the seductive vacation dreams of others, such as your workers. However...

...if you are on the workers side of this equation, then it's really simple what is more than likely happening to you:

You are probably being owned.

So, from this moment forward, when your eyes open from your slumber, ask yourself: *"Am I being owned?"*

REMEMBER: It's no longer entrepreneurship by option. It's now entrepreneurship by necessity.

Chapter 2:

"What Is Your 'It?' Who Are Your 'They?'"

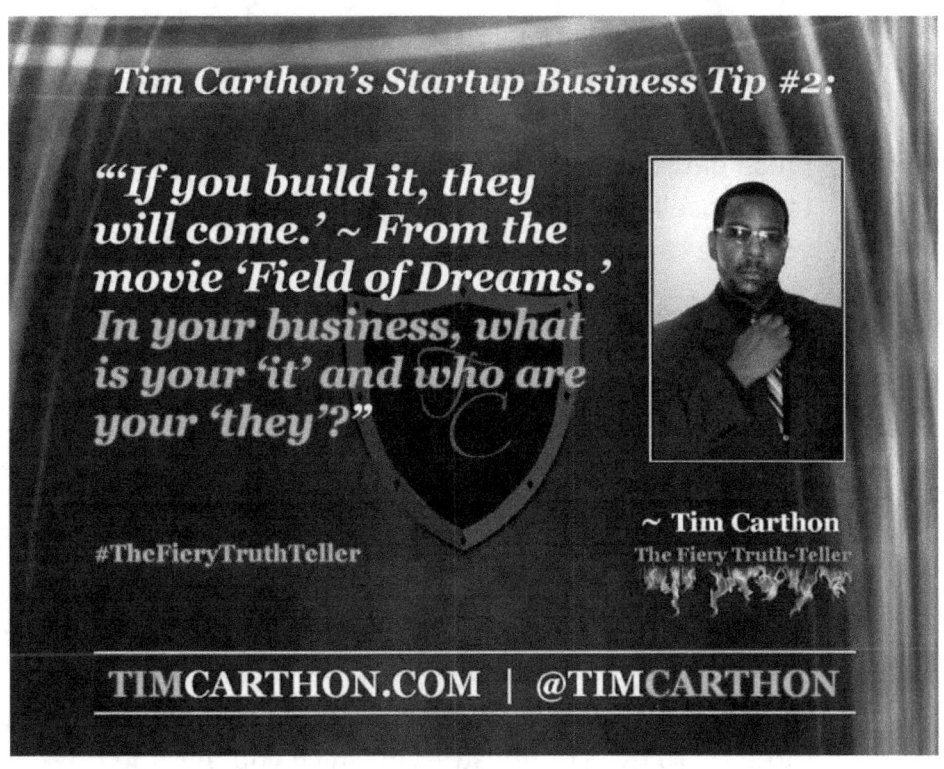

One of the most important things in business, if not *the* most important thing, is identity; knowing what it is that your business offers product/service-wise. Another important thing is *knowing your customer base.*

Businesses thrive by the symbiotic relationship between those two things; customers purchasing products and services and the profits companies make from selling their base those products and services. The latter cannot be done without the former, so you, as an entrepreneur, have to find out a few simple things prior to you starting your business:

1.) **In what industries do you wish to primarily spend the rest of your life?** Ever had a job where your work involved you sitting in a cubicle for 8 hours a day? How much did you enjoy that? What about a job going door-to-door selling a product you wouldn't use yourself? Did you love that job?

    There is nothing worse than living a life doing something career-wise that you absolutely loathe. You tend to spend most of your downtime thinking about how you wish you could do something else. Then something even worse happens. Eventually you've been there for so long that you end up getting a promotion.

    So now you're even deeper into a career you hate; one out of which you want so desperately to get. When starting a business, you want to make sure that you pick three (3) to five (5) industries in which you feel you'd love to live your entire life; industries in which you believe you would not only thrive financially, but also spiritually.

2.) **What need does that industry have or what void is there to fill?** Once you pick your industries, you need to take a closer look at the first/primary industry and see where it is you can fit in. What product can you offer? What service do they need?

If you brainstorm for a long time over days, weeks, months (*however long you think you need*) and realize there is no place you can find for you in that industry, then move to your second/secondary industry and repeat the brainstorming.

If you cannot find a fit there either, then do the same brainstorming method for the next few industries. Trust me, you will find a void that you can fill. It will either be a new product or service or an upgrade of an existing product or service.

3.) **Is filling that need/void feasible?** Once you've realized what the industry you've selected needs, you have to ask yourself if being able to offer that product or service to the customers in that industry is even feasible?

If it is, it may take a smaller amount of energy and a shorter amount of time or a larger amount of energy during a longer timeframe to fully develop that product or service. All of that comes into play and *should* be decided upon before you commit to the industry you've selected and create or enhance a product/service for it.

4.) ***Who is it that can benefit the most from your products and services?*** Now that you've selected your industry and the products and/or services you will be initially selling/offering, you have to find your target market; the individuals to whom you will mainly be advertising to buy those products and/or services.

Target markets are based on a host of things ranging from age and income to education, gender, and race. Knowing the specifics of the individuals to whom you want to sell your newly developed products and/or services can be the difference in a profitable quarter or one that bankrupts your company.

REMEMBER: Now that you've selected where you want to spend your business career, the void you wish to fill in that industry, and the people you will be primarily servicing, you are now free to start the development of your actual products and services. Happy entrepreneuring!

Chapter 3:

"Your Unstoppable Digital Juggernaut."

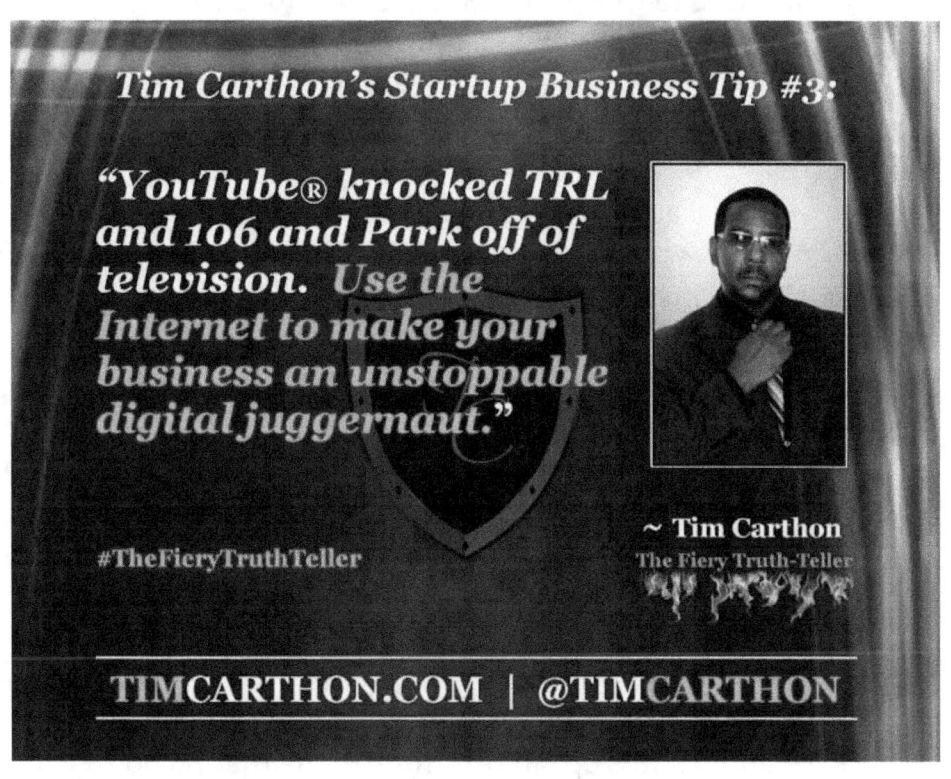

One thing that I've learned in the past 14 years of my business life is that perception can be as important as reality. I learned that, in the videos that music artists make, the cars, jewelry, and houses are most of the time not even owned by them.

They're rented.

The reason they rent them is because of what perception can do for an artist/brand/company and their/its bottom line.

Rich athletes hang out with other rich athletes. Why? Because they don't have to worry about them asking for anything because they already know that a.) They either don't need it because they have it already or b.) They have enough money to get it themselves if they want.

When a musical artist is perceived as being wealthy (*something in which those façade videos tremendously aid*), it can start an extremely lucrative chain of events:

1.) The videos stir up interest from fans.

2.) That interest aids tremendously in the selling of their music.

3.) That, in turn, makes other wealthy people and celebrities want to hang around the artist.

4.) Interest from fans and solidified wealthy individuals and celebrities stirs up interest from journalists and book publishers.

5.) Articles and books written and published by those journalists and book publishers stir up interest from television directors who and studios that make television shows and made-for-TV movies.

6.) Subsequently, those television shows and TV movies, and how well they are received, can catch the eye of a movie studio that may approach them to do a major motion picture.

So, as you can see, perception, in the right context, can be just as important as reality, depending on for what it is used. The Internet, just like a music video, can be used to start a series of chain-reactions that lead to a highly lucrative ending, and a lot of it, if not most of it, can be based off of pure perception.

On the Internet, you can look just as big as a company that has been in existence for 70 years, but you've only been in existence for 7 months. Their CEO walks around in their corporate office in a $3,000 suit, whereas you walk around in your corporate office, which happens to double as your second bedroom, in your boxer briefs underwear.

And guess what?

It doesn't matter.

The only thing that the billions of people on the Internet see is what you want them to see, which, if you're smart, are the products and/or services you're offering.

Remember: It was not long ago that the Internet was not readily available to the majority of this country, let alone half the world. People, especially in this country, tend to have a short attention span and convenient amnesia.

The Internet allowed for a digital revolution unlike anything we'd ever seen. Some long-standing companies (*even companies older than 70 years*) were able to adjust their business plans in order to be successful in the new digital age. The New York Times®, the world's foremost and said to be most trusted newspaper, was one of them.

When the digital revolution came, it was only a matter of time before the newspaper industry would suffer industry-crippling customer and monetary losses. Their smart business strategy of getting ahead of the crumbling newspaper industry and upgrading from paper-only to both paper and digital copy kept their newspaper not just alive, but thriving in the new digital age. However…

…others, who were not paying attention, weren't so lucky.

Netflix®, which is an Internet-streaming video service, got ahead of the digital streaming revolution by thinking about what their customers wanted *first* in order to boost profits *second*:

- Easy access to videos.
- Not having to leave the house to go rent a movie.
- Not having to leave the house just to drop a movie back off.
- No late fees.

Chapter 3: Your Unstoppable Digital Juggernaut.

Yet Blockbuster® video was so stuck on profits that they forgot to give the customers what they wanted:

- Easy access to videos.
- Not having to leave the house to go rent a movie.
- Not having to leave the house just to drop a movie back off.
- No late fees.

Now Blockbuster® is a shell of its former self and offers the same service as Netflix®, but no one knows. Why not? Because no one cares any longer. That is, probably in large part, because people still have nightmares about jumping in the car in their pajamas at night trying to make it to their video store before midnight just to keep from being charged a ridiculous $2.50 late fee.

It's as though people are basking in the karma of Blockbuster's demise due to their perceived greed, yet Netflix's stock price is over $102[2] and you can access any of their television shows and movies from any digital device that has Internet access.

Simply put, what the Internet did was level the playing field for big and small businesses. Like I said, you can look just as big as a company that has been in existence for 70 years, but you've only been in existence for 7 months.

This is the power of the Internet.

It gives you access to billions of people, and, if your products and/or services are up to par, an opportunity to really compete with companies 100xs your startup's size in order to try and make those billions your customers.

REMEMBER: All you have to do is tailor-make your products and/or services well, select your customer base well, tailor-make your pitch message well, tailor-make your advertisement well, and then go, go, go!

Make necessary, smart adjustments along the way and you will have the best chance at growing your business and making it a serious force with which to be reckoned on and off the Internet.

Chapter 4:

"8 Hours a Day Keeps Success Away."

There is an extraordinary video that went viral which featured "The Hip-Hop Preacher." His real name is Eric Thomas, PhD (*also known as 'ET'*) and he is a speaker, educator, author, activist, and minister.[3]

He spoke about how there was a young man who wanted to be as successful as one older man. The older man told the younger man to meet him at the beach the next morning if he wanted to be successful.

The young man met him the next morning and was taught an important lesson about the depths of what it takes to be successful. Later on in the video when 'ET' was talking to the audience, he made a profound statement that is the epitome of about what this chapter is.

Sacrifice.

Whenever I train people business infrastructure-wise, there are several specific points from which all other decisions should derive. The most important point is that when one enters the business owner realm, they have to, if they haven't already, make a serious shift in their mentality.

Part of that shift is the understanding that, as a business owner, there are things in your life that are extremely valuable to you that are going to have to be sacrificed. One of those things:

Sleep.

Chapter 4: 8 Hours a Day Keeps Success Away.

Just think about it: 11pm EST. The ultra comfortable posturepedic bed with the super soft, but form-fitting posturepedic pillow and the comforter that makes you feel like you're happily drowning in rest's perfection. It is the only thing about which you can think after a hard, draining day of work.

Your body is fatigued.
Your mind, not so much.

After preparing for it, you climb onto this fluffy sea of a mattress, primed to let it engulf you in it and the peaceful dreams it has in store for you.

Your body begins to power down.
Your eyes close.

Your mind consciously wanders, until conscious thoughts seamlessly merge into dreams. 6:30am EST, the sound of birds chirping repeatedly awakens you from your sleeping beauty-like slumber.

7 ½ hours of restful, peaceful sleep.

Well guess what? WAKE THE HELL UP!

Starting a business *ain't no fairytale*. Sacrificing ain't no fairytale. They're the opposite of 'Neverland®.' Both can be difficult, frustrating, time-consuming, and maddening. They can bring you to the brink of bankruptcy, only to give you a stay of financial execution just so they can both inevitably torture you again sooner than you'd like.

There is something that I created some time ago called The Checkmark Theory™. This theory is simple. Where you are is point "A." If you wish to start a business, more than likely the sacrifices you're going to have to make are going to lose you things that you love, maybe even people, too. However...

...when you master sacrificing...when you accept your losses and they become like gnats where you can just brush them away as though the bite didn't hurt at all, no matter how hard, that is when you reach the letter "B."

This is when you have become the person who you need to be in order to take your business to the height of success you believe it deserves...level "C"; a height that far surpasses what you had when you started.

Tim Carthon's Checkmark Theory™

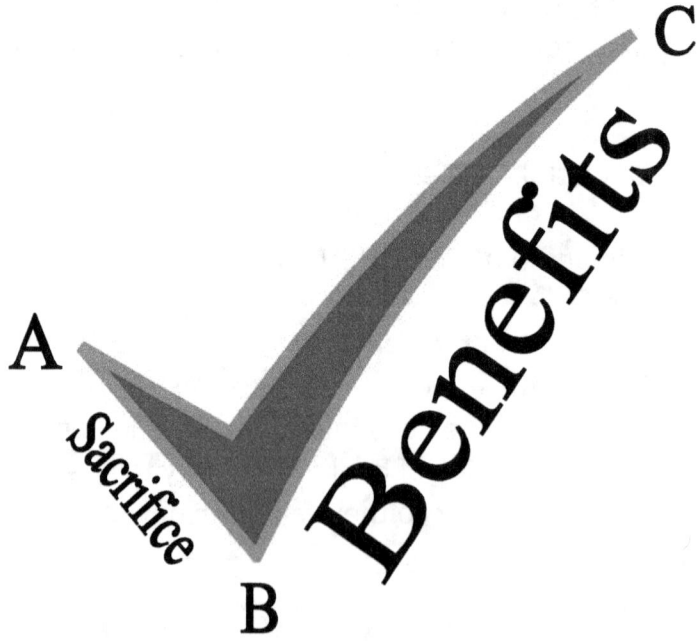

Chapter 4: 8 Hours a Day Keeps Success Away.

Unfortunately, so many people are absolutely terrified of the initial "A-to-B" drop that the "B-to-C" rise can't even overcome that fear, and that is understandable.

Starting a business is a female dog that's in heat and wants to screw you royally, and there are only certain ways that you can minimize the beatings, all of which include sacrificing. However…

…one way to minimize the beatings is to significantly increase your business hours for maximum time usage efficiency. To do that, you have to be willing to sacrifice a chunk of your oh-so-happy nightly drowning; something that seemingly most people are not willing to do. I'll let the Hip-Hop Preacher explain this as well:

> *"Most of you don't want success as much as you wanna sleep. Some of you love sleep more than you love success, and I'm here to tell you today if you're going to be successful, you've gotta be willing to give up sleep. You've gotta be willing to work off of 3 hours of sleep, 2 hours, if you really wanna be successful, some days, you're goin' have to stay up 3 days in a row. Then you'll be successful."*[(4)] ~ Eric Thomas

REMEMBER: Sacrificing and starting a business *ain't no fairytale*. However, finishing building a successful one definitely will be.

TIM CARTHON
WWW.TIMCARTHON.COM

Chapter 5:

"Customer Service is Not Dead, Right?"

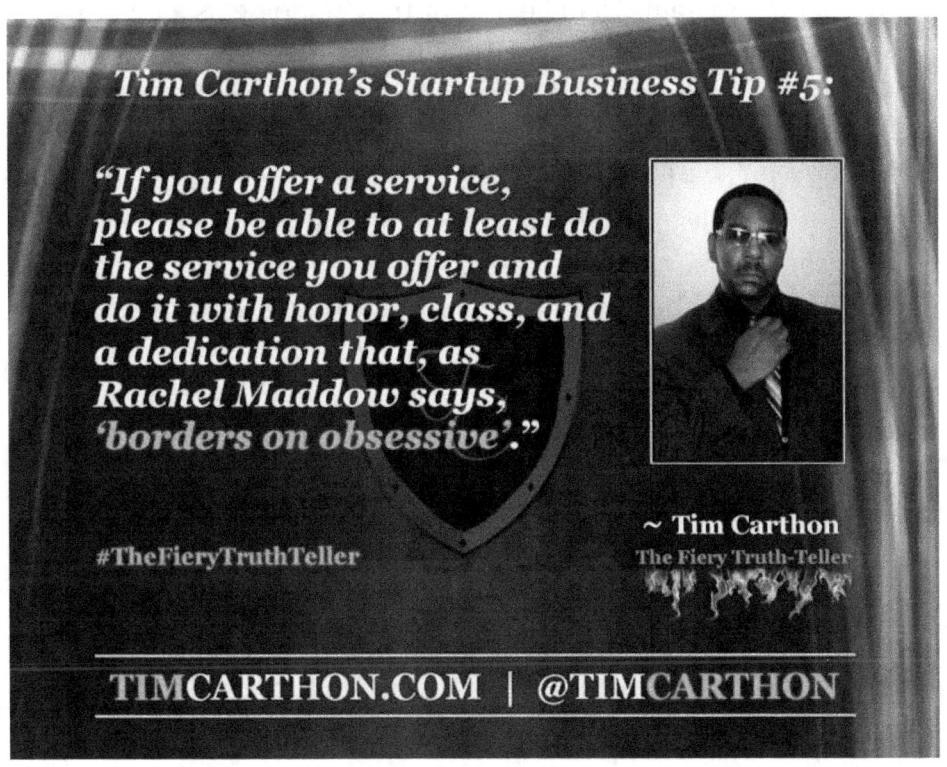

One thing that has been seemingly completely lost in today's business world is customer service. You can say it's because of how people raised the generation who are now our fast food workers, customer representatives, bank tellers, etc., and you might be right. Hell, you're probably right.

Growing up, I was taught to be thoughtful and kind to individuals. I was taught to look out for others; helping them as much as I could when they were in need.

Today, it is as though the generation who is in the position to now serve us seems to believe that they're doing us a favor by serving us, forgetting that 1.) They're being paid to do so, and 2.) Businesses run off of the profit they make *from* us.

So, since no one is forcing patrons to come to or buy at that store, it is a privilege for the store to have these patrons in it. They could be somewhere else contemplating spending their hard-earned money, but no. Here they are at a store with great products, but completely lousy customer service.

I KNOW you know exactly about what I'm talking right now, right?

These types of customer service workers make customers feel unhappy, unwanted, and unappreciated. When that happens, not only is money lost when the customer walks out, but reputation and more money are lost when that used-to-be customer spreads the word about how terrible they were treated in your establishment.

This is why training and company culture are so important, and all of which starts with you, the entrepreneur who started the business. So here are a few quick tips to help build 5-star rated, phenomenal customer service:

1.) Do not start offering services until you have, on some level, a mastery of the service you're offering. Nothing is worse to people spending their money than to be ready to spend it on something only to find out that the person offering it is a novice and is showing it, especially in specialty services. Learn the craft, at least to the point of above-average coherency, and THEN sell the product(s)/service(s). Simple.

2.) *Upscale*, as far as *brand quality*, is always a plus for customers. When building your brand, you have to treat customers with the care with which you would treat precious jewels. Even though some of them are rough around the edges, you understand completely the value of them anyway. Like a haircut for a man turns his confidence dial up, so does being treated like you matter.

   In other words, do classy work for your customers with a level of care and honor that would make chivalrous medieval knights proud and your bank accounts will reward you with plentiful bounty.

3.) You ever had a conversation about a sports team and everyone in the conversation started naming players? If so, did you ever notice that, when someone named a particular player, everyone in the conversation said something like, "*Yeeeeeeeeeeeeeah! Now THEY can play!*"? Everyone was in *positive* agreement not just on that individual's skill, but also their will.

A towering, facts-based, completely sweet journalist named Rachel Maddow was talking about her journalistic devotion to the *"disparate facts"* and *"finding their coherence."* She explained how *"Doing this right takes rigor and a devotion to facts that borders on obsessive."* From her repeatedly detailed and factually-based journalism, I have no doubt about any of those statements.

When doing a job, especially one that is customer service-based, it is imperative that your focus on and dedication to doing the best job that you can be extremely high. It should be so high that you *positively* stand out to your customers, especially in conversation, just like how Rachel Maddow *positively* stands out to television news viewers for her integrity and dedication to her craft.

REMEMBER: Do not start offering services until you have, on some level, a mastery of the service you're offering, do classy work for your customers with a level of care and honor that would make chivalrous medieval knights proud, and your bank accounts will reward you with plentiful bounty, and be certain that your focus on and dedication to doing the best job that you can do are extremely high.

Chapter 6:

"Feast on Facts, Not Feelings."

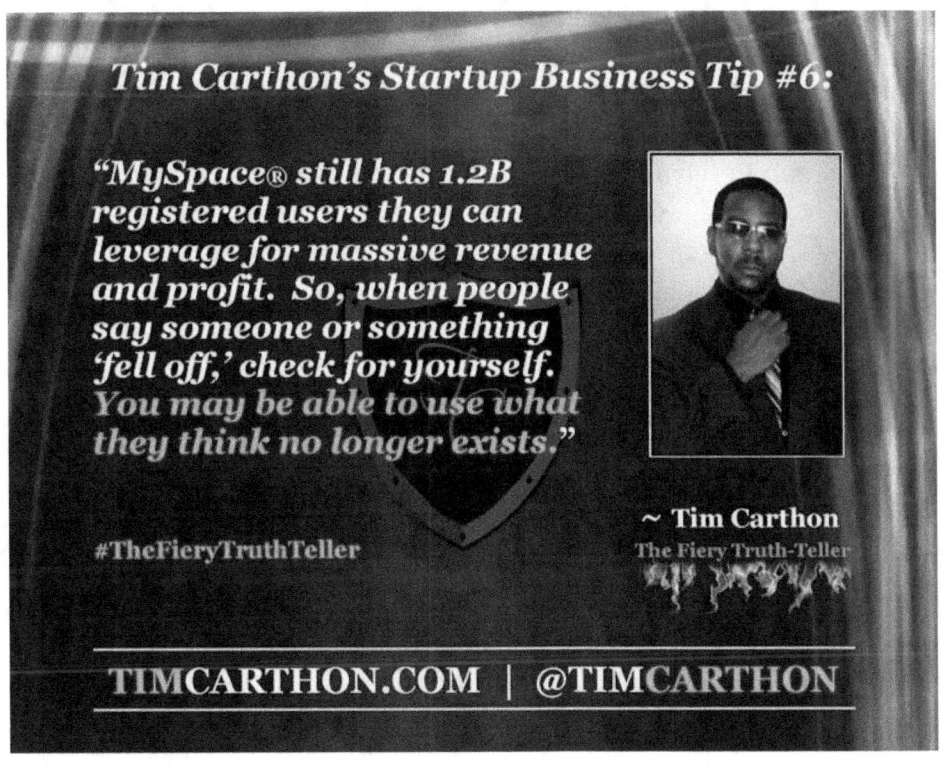

It's almost always cringe-worthy when someone mentions a 'used-to-be-awesome' person or thing. It's as though the people in the room look at that thing as a 'used to be hot' rapper who no longer deserves to even be mentioned in conversations.

Forget the fact that the person or the thing made a ton of money, garnered a lot of influence, maybe even changed the nature of their industry for decades or even centuries to come, and may even still be doing so behind the scenes. It seemingly just doesn't matter anymore.

Take the once go-to social media site MySpace.com. No doubt that a ton of things went wrong for MySpace®; from what MySpace's vice-president of online marketing from 2009 to 2011 Sean Percival said was one of MySpace's main failings:

> *"Bloat, with verticals covering celebrity, fashion, sport and even books"*[5] to just an outright awful user-to-user interaction experience.

Unfortunately for them, the biggest thing that went wrong was Facebook®.

Fast-forward to the most recent year, Facebook® has a whopping over 1.55B monthly users and over 1B daily users[6] with revenues of over $17.9B[7] while MySpace® reports up-to 50M unique views a month and provides marketers with access to its over 1.2B registered users.[8]

Chapter 6: Feast on Facts, Not Feelings.

It's now an entertainment-focused site that plays music videos and songs, but none of that is obviously relevant to the doubters...or is it?

Do we even know if the individuals shunning them have this pertinent information about this supposed used-to-be-awesome thing? That's a legitimate question, seeing as though people tend to latch on to the rumor faster than they do the researched information, and who can blame them?

Rumors are naughty, even borderline salacious, so they're intellectually tasty, but so is sugar, and we know how bad that is for our bodies, right?

This is where understanding that facts and research play an even bigger role in business than rumors and innuendo. Although MySpace® is no longer the worldwide juggernaut it used to be, Time, Inc. understood the power of the network that it built over the years and decided to leverage it.

In 2016, they purchased MySpace's parent company Viant® and expects $100M in ad revenue from its user database.[9]

How's that for *"used-to-be-awesome"*?

You didn't know MySpace® could still generate $100M in ad revenue, did you? More than likely you didn't. That's because facts don't travel the world as fast as rumor, especially positive ones.

What do you think would happen if rumor was that MySpace® was shutting down? Do you think no one would have heard about it or would it have been all over the network news outlets? Easily the latter.

Too many times people focus on what they hear about where the political, entertainment, or business winds seem to be shifting based on rumors instead of the direct facts of the actual weather from vetted, veteran weather analysts.

When you do that, you place yourself in a position to miss out on opportunities that you never even knew were available. However, someone or something, like Time, Inc., will see that opportunity and pick it up swiftly, and don't you think you deserve better than to lose opportunities in that manner?

REMEMBER: Always listen to and hear the information given, but don't do 'group think.' Be an individual and always think and do research for yourself. That's the most powerful you that you will ever be.

Chapter 7:

"Being 'Better' Over Being 'Bigger.'"

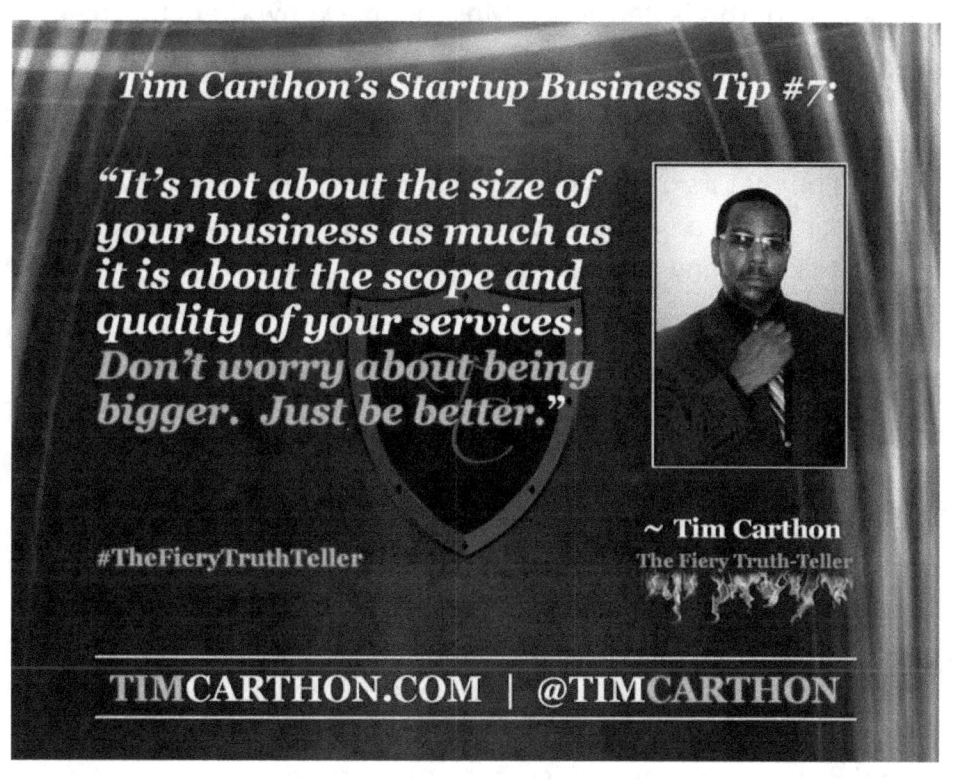

There have been so many times in life where I heard about companies that used to be simple "Mom and Pop" stores, which catered to its customers with homemade products and hometown service, all of a sudden being swallowed up by *bigger capitalism*. That bigger capitalism's name:

Corporate conglomerate.

Now what is a corporate conglomerate? A corporate conglomerate is a company that has a number of different companies that form a whole but remain distinct entities.[10] An example of this is PepsiCo®. Most people know them for their signature drink Pepsi®.

So let's say that one day you get angry at Pepsi® for something. It can be that its owner said something you didn't like, that the company gave a political donation to a candidate who you didn't like, or any other reason.

In either case, you decided that you're not going to buy Pepsi® anymore. So, the next time you walk into a store, you past the Pepsi® bottle and decide to get a Mountain Dew® instead.

That'll teach Pepsi® to piss off consumers, right?

So you've made a stand by no longer supporting Pepsi®, or so you thought. What you didn't know is that PepsiCo® also owns their 'supposed' rivals Mountain Dew®.[11] PepsiCo® *absorbed* Mountain Dew® into its conglomerate like the Borg from Star Trek® absorbs other species into its collective.

I know all you Trekkies appreciate that I referred to the Borg as 'its' and not 'their,' seeing as though all of its pieces work as one. It's the same way with a corporate conglomerate. All of its parts work toward one thing:

Profit for the parent company.

With Mom and Pop stores, profit is important, as it is with any business, but their focus is usually more on customer service, as they live in the community and have to see the people they service daily.

Those two pieces of the puzzle are what help the M&P stores to create and maintain prime products and services for their customers, which creates a demand for them; helping to build their business' notoriety and subsequent profits.

That, in turn, leads to big companies coming in and making these M&P stores large monetary offers to buy all aspects of their businesses; offers that these community store owners almost can't refuse.

Those big companies then take those same M&Ps and turn them into profitable national and even international brands. However, the brands lose a large portion of their luster because they lose something else in the swift transition from a small store to a gargantuan brand.

The homemade touch.

No, I'm not saying that companies should not want to expand and grow to the size of a corporate behemoth, but no company should ever sacrifice that which made it what it is purely for profit.

REMEMBER: When you decide to build, grow, and then expand your business, build swiftly and efficiently, but grow slowly and boldly and make sure that all aspects of what made you great and unique are taught and improved at every point. This way, you maintain the integrity of not only your products and services, but your soon-to-be international brand.

Chapter 8:

"Money = Influence."

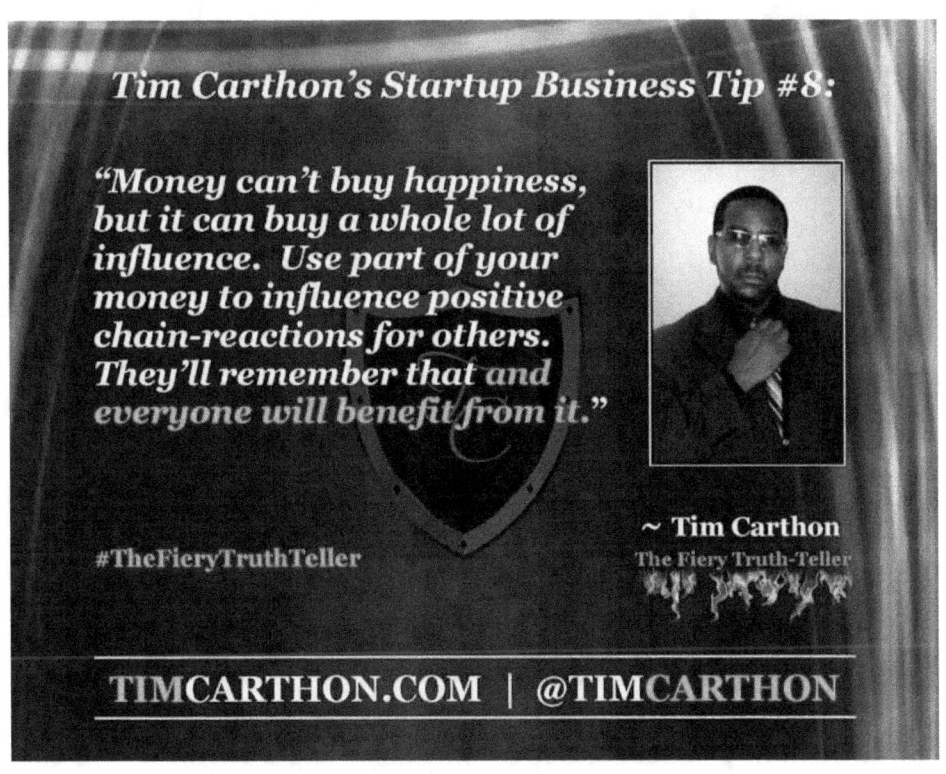

Charity.

Most people know of someone who or some entity that has been either monetarily charitable to another person or has given generously to a charitable entity, usually a non-profit organization.

This act has been universally seen historically as an act of generosity. In more recent decades, it has come to be seen as an act of selfishness, depending on if you are or are not a gargantuan corporation.

In industrialized societies, corporations tend to be given tax breaks for a multitude of business spending decisions ranging from company reinvestment to charitable giving. Those breaks are used to lower the tax burden of a company in order to help the company sustain or grow capital.

This, in turn, is supposed to spur investment in the community from the corporations by way of employment for residents of those communities in which the corporations, or one of their branches, reside.

Corporations taking advantage of most of the tax breaks they're afforded tend to be seen by the masses for its face value. If a company invests in a building or new furniture, it's rare that you will find someone who thinks that the reason they bought the building or the furniture was for a tax break.

The company needs a place from which to operate and sometimes that space needs to be expanded, hence a new building. And a more appealing facility can breed a better return on client solicitation investment and employee turnover ratios.

Makes sense, right? However...

...when it comes to charitable giving, a lot of times that generosity is seen as a *low-key power move*.

Let's take publicly traded companies for example. Charities are usually found to have been structured as a *non-profit organization*. This means that their formation was not intended to generate profits as much as it was to aid communities and/or communal entities through some form of program, service, product, monetary donation, or a combination of them.

Publicly traded companies have what is called a "fiduciary responsibility" (*or duty*) to their shareholders or "principals." Although the legal definition of 'fiduciary responsibility/duty' is *a legal duty to act solely in another party's interests*,[12] in layman's terms it translates with publicly traded corporations to, "*No matter what, make us as much money as you can!*"

Since publicly traded companies have that fiduciary responsibility, them giving to charities tends to be looked upon by the masses not as an act of generosity, but selfishness. The public tends to see it as another way for the corporation to lower their own tax burden. However...

...since these large corporations have this money to give, it tends to influence the individuals who and entities to which they give these large donations. That influence buys good will through press releases, commercial spots, logo placement, local, regional, and national media interviews, and more from those charities to which these publicly traded companies give.

Look at the late great Michael Jackson. Michael Jackson was one of the most charitable *individual* givers in the history of the world. He gave well over $100M to charities in his lifetime[13] and his estate is still doing so.

The amount of help and positive energy that these charities have been able to give to this world is probably immeasurable, in large part because of financially-well off and generous individuals like the 'King of Pop.'

At his fame's height, when he spoke, media swarmed. When he announced a performance, markets moved. Where he performed, economies boomed. His music and its influence were, and still are, world renowned.

Is it any wonder that Michael Jackson was one of the most influential *non-politicians* in the world?

Music and money are powerful. In the business world, the perception of power drives influence. However, in the age of social media, power is no longer money-based-only for the rich such as Michael Jackson, but access-based-also for the masses.

With social media sites like YouTube®, Twitter®, Facebook®, and Instagram®, power and the ability to influence and galvanize the masses, which was normally reserved for society's elite, has now also been put into the hands of social

Chapter 8: Money = Influence.

media account-holding Internet 'celebrities' who have garnered hundreds of thousands to millions of followers.

Many of these individuals now take their followers and use them to the advantage of society as a whole, not just themselves as budding entrepreneurs. This gives them a level of influence that was not available to them before the Internet. However...

...unlike Michael Jackson, most of the individuals on these social networks are not rich, so, although more powerful than previously, their influence is limited.

Now take the individuals who have built profitable businesses, but also have a large social media following, like 20-time Grammy® Award Winning Songstress Beyonce' Knowles, better known as just *Beyonce*.[14] Her influence is a little different, to say the least.

From political situations to entertainment, with a net worth of $450M[15] Beyonce has the actual capital to *literally* buy influence. Just on those four aforementioned social media sites, she has over a 148M fan following. Mix all of that with the 31 charities to which she gives, including...

- The American Foundation for AIDS Research
- The Boys & Girls Clubs of America
- The Global Poverty Project
- The Kids Wish Network
- The Miami Children's Hospital Foundation
- The Save The Music Foundation, and Stand Up To Cancer[16]

...and she can set fashion trends by advertising something on her social media or, if she *really* wants to be bold, get massive, world-wide race relations and climate change conversations started by simply doing an interview where she *alludes* to issues ranging from systemic racism to potential environmental disaster.

Is it any surprise that Beyonce is one of the most beloved celebrities in the world?

REMEMBER: Influence from having a massive social media following online is effective, but influence from money, especially the charitable giving of it, is much more powerful. However...

...mix the two and you can become an unstoppable force of business profit influence and good will, at least as long as you're making that profit and using it for such, and the world will be a better place because of you.

Chapter 9:

"A Little Caring. A Lot of Cash."

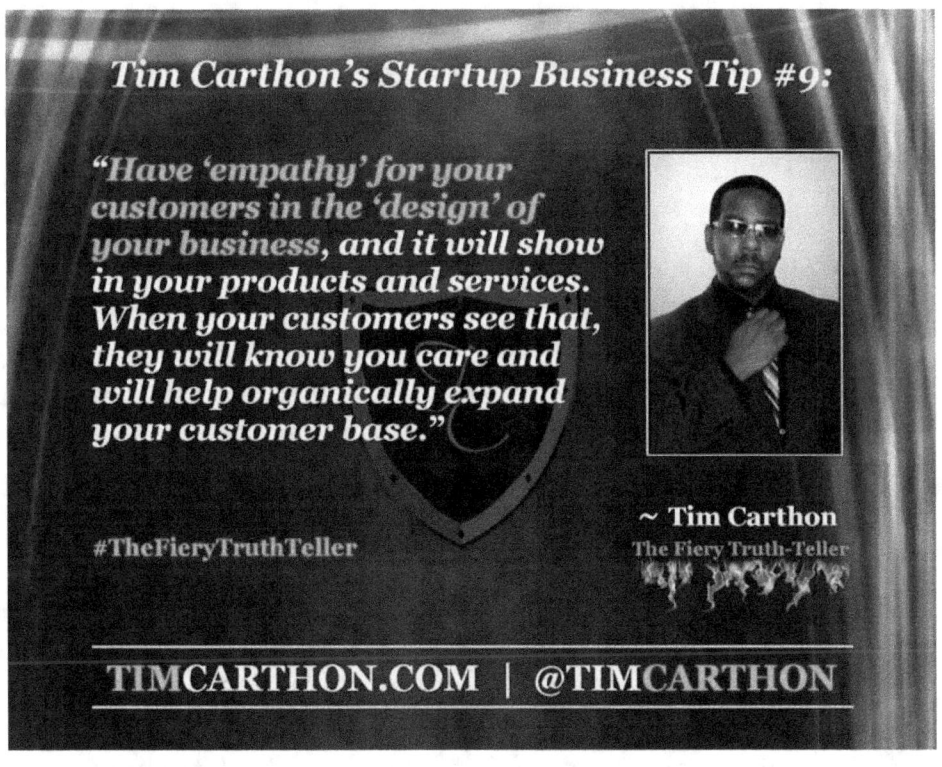

How did it feel when you came up with your business? Exciting? Exhilarating? Scary? All of the above? Of course it did. Starting a business is a life-changing proposition. The question is, why did you create your business?

- Did you create it because you wanted to do something for others?
- Did you create it because you wanted to make a profit off of selling a new or current product?
- Or maybe you wanted to make a ton of money off of selling your expertise?

Wait.

Have you even come up with your business?

Whatever the case, one thing that you need to understand about creating a business is that initially a lot of what you do during the development stage is going to be, if even not purposely, *emotionally-based*. That simply means that you're going to be making decisions based off of how you feel in your heart. That is a dangerous proposition, if done based on that alone.

In basketball, there are several aspects to an individual's game; dribbling, passing, blocking, jumping, dunking, shooting, defending, 'posting up,' etc. There were people who came through the professional realm and were amazing dunkers. There were other individuals who came through those same realms and weren't great dunkers, but were absolute sharp-shooters from 'beyond the arc.'

Chapter 9: A Little Caring. A Lot of Cash.

Then there were those rare individuals; those who could shoot it from the three-point line, defend like no other, jump through the rafters, dunk from the free throw line, consistently complete behind-the-back no-look passes, and more. These were the game changers. These were the all-time greats.

All of these players were definitely amazing in their respective rights. However, history books are written more about and heavily favor those who excel in almost every aspect of the sport individually, not just one.

REMEMBER: When you create your business, you want to use a combination of what's in your heart for your business and how it can be branded in order to give the people you're trying to serve exactly what they need.

That will not only get them to come back for you to serve them again and again, but it will also get them to spread the word about the greatness of you and what you offer.

And that attitude and approach is an even more potent, positively-dangerous business proposition that can inevitably make your life and the lives of the people you serve wealthier.

Chapter 10:

"'Employer -vs.- Employee' Thinking."

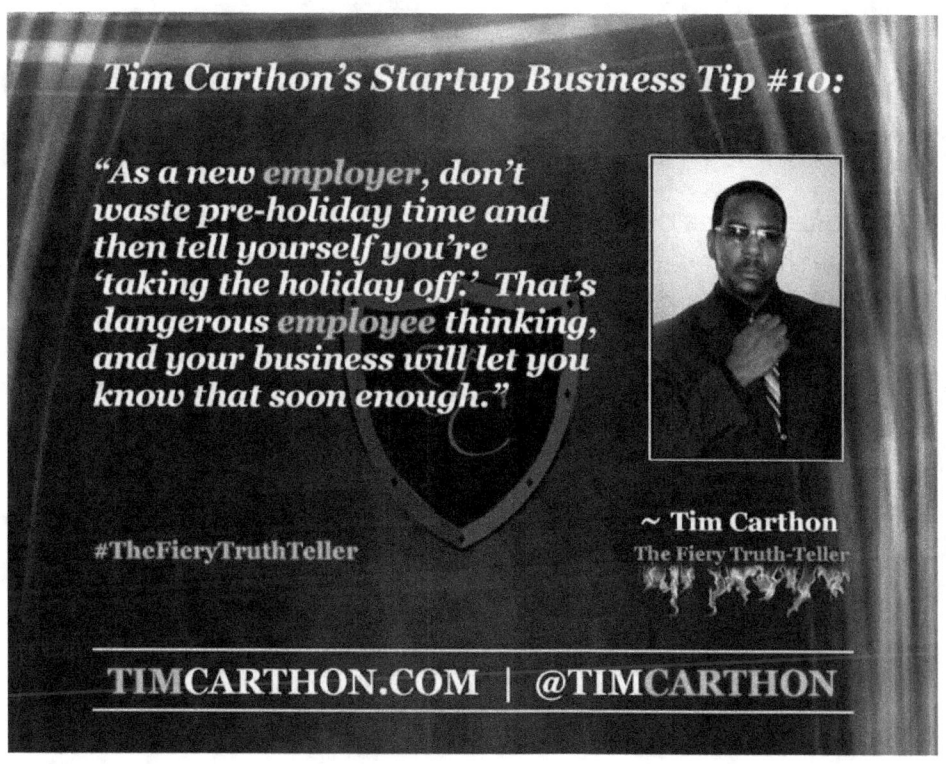

Have you ever seen a person who gets a refund check, be it a tax refund or a Student loan refund, and they all of a sudden are acting as though they're the richest person in the world? They take that money and go buy new, shiny things that help make other people really rich, all the while not truly investing in their own potential wealth.

It's one thing if what it is they were buying somehow translated to helping them with their plans for the future. It's, however, a completely different thing when they're making 'status purchases;' purchases made to keep up or enhance an image.

Even then, if keeping up or enhancing an image is somehow directly tied to their future success, then that would be considered an investment and not a true status purchase.

Too many times the decisions of individuals are counter-productive to everything they say they want. People want a car, but they don't save their money or build their credit. People say they want to get married, but they never learn how the gender they wish to marry works and to make the appropriate adjustments for such.

People say that they want to start a successful business, but the minute they start the business they want to move forward in the same manner they were when they were working a 9-5pm job for another company.

Big mistake.

Being an employee is a completely different world from being an employer. It's like the difference between being a Principal and being a teacher. Yes, both Principals and teachers have tons of work that have to be done on a daily basis. However...

...there is a difference in the type and level of that work. Teachers have to worry about themselves, their classrooms, and their Students. Principals have to worry about themselves, the building, school lunches, books, every staff member, every classroom, every Student, and their parents.

Teachers are the employees. Principals are the employers. If the employer doesn't do their job well, it makes it more difficult for the employee to do their job and for the school to survive, let alone thrive.

This is the same principle regarding new entrepreneurs. Here's a true, personal story showing the importance of this principle:

How Bad Did He Want to Breathe? The Story of 'The Unexpected Entrepreneur'

A few years ago, I helped a friend of mine start a new business using formulas that I'd developed over, at the time, 12 years. He'd worked for others for years, but was fired from his job the year his business was started.

I told him that was the best thing that ever happened to him.

He couldn't understand my happiness at his seeming demise, but his understanding of it was irrelevant. I didn't need his understanding for him to start his business. I only needed his agreement and cooperation. The understanding of my happiness about him being fired would come in due time.

I explained to him that this was the perfect time to start his business, so, trusting me, he decided to allow me, almost immediately after he was let go from his job, to help him develop his business.

Now, although the services from his business weren't new, the concepts behind the reason for and the delivery of the services were absolutely brilliant. They were based off of the things he'd been doing for the past 25 years of his life, including at his now *previous* job. However...

...owning a business is not a 9am-5pm job. It's almost a 9am-9am job, at least at the beginning stages of growth.

For months, I tried to get him to understand that there were significant changes that he had to make to his work ethic in order to compensate for the shift in work load...the shift, in essence, from teacher to Principal. This was in part due to the total difference in time and effort needed for his new venture versus his old job.

Unfortunately he didn't follow my lead. Instead...

1.) He'd go to sleep at 11:30pm.

2.) He would wake up at 10am and not be ready for the day until noon.

Chapter 10: 'Employer -vs.- Employee' Thinking.

3.) He opened the wrong type of bank account because he didn't take the details/specifics of instructions seriously.

4.) He wouldn't learn his control panel for his company domain names.

5.) He wouldn't learn his emailing system for his company emails.

6.) He wouldn't post on his company social media accounts or his website.

7.) He'd repeatedly take days off to do nothing productive.

8.) He'd travel out of town for fun with his family almost every weekend.

9.) He'd take people's word for it that they have an agreement on a business deal, and then stop working on any other deals based off of their 'word.'

10.) He'd give himself an out for anything he didn't like, whether that out be someone else doing it or him giving repeated excuses for it just not getting done.

Whatever he did and whenever he did it, it was almost always the mindset of the employee that he *used to be* making decisions instead of the employer that he was *trying to be*. That, in turn, had devastating consequences on his business:

1.) By him going to sleep at 11:30pm, he was wasting valuable time at night that he could be using to get work done while the majority of the actual country was 'on pause.'

2.) By him waking up at 10am and not being ready for the day until noon, the people to whom he needed to speak and who he needed to see the most were not as available. That's because they were mostly available between 8:30-10:30am.

That, in turn, slowed down his ROR (*Rate of Return*) or ROI (*Return on Investment*) for his business. And, due to the time-sensitive nature of his business' industry, it had crushing consequences year over year (*YOY*) for his bottom line.

3.) By him opening the *wrong* type of bank account, he had to open another one that had the *correct* bank account type. Unfortunately, he couldn't close the first one for six (6) months because that was one of the account rules. Another rule was a high account maintenance fee that his company had to pay; money out of the figurative window every month for absolutely nothing *special* that was helping his business.

4.) By him not learning his control panel for his company domain names, a series of chain-reactions occurred. We'd initially set the payment for his domain names up with the first bank account he opened that turned out to be the wrong account type.

By him not knowing how his control panel worked, he couldn't log in to change the banking information for his domain names. That meant that, when his hosting company tried to pull payment for his domains the next year, they were trying to pull it from an account that no longer existed.

After trying that for so long, the hosting company just shut down his website. Unfortunately, my friend didn't know for days that his website was shut down because he didn't check his website or control panel on a daily basis. And, when he found out, there was nothing he could do to fix it except call me. Why? Because he did not learn his control panel like he was instructed.

Luckily for him, I just so happened to be in town when it happened and there with him, so I fixed the issue swiftly. However, the situation left pertinent questions:

- How many people tried to visit his website while it was down?
- Worse than that, who were the people trying to visit?
- Were they influential?
- Did his website being down make him miss a huge business opportunity?

In other words, how much damage had been done to his reputation just from his site being shut down for days?

5.) By him not learning his email system for his company, when neither I nor his assistant were available, he didn't know what to do. He ended up missing deadlines and sending out terribly flawed emails. How much damage did he do to his and his company's reputations by missing those deadlines and sending out faulty emails?

6.) By him not posting on his social media accounts (*which he only neglected for about six [6] months*), he had people visiting his pages, but there was absolutely no up-to-date content.

The only content that was on his pages was telling people that his services were "Coming soon...", and those were done by me months in advance. His last post's timestamp would say "2 months ago." He finally began posting to his social media accounts when one day after rehearsal one of his Students came up to him and said:

> "I thought you said that we would be on the Internet? I went to your page, but I didn't see any pictures of us."

That's when it hit him that everything I'd been telling him about how people look at him and his company social media-wise when he doesn't see them was true. Too bad he wasted time (*and probably some legitimacy in many people's eyes*) waiting to find out the hard way. However...

...that wasn't as bad as what he did, or rather didn't do, with the website.

Even after he had rehearsals and events, he didn't post any photos from those rehearsals or events on his

Chapter 10: 'Employer -vs.- Employee' Thinking.

website for two (2) years.

No, you didn't read that wrong.

He posted no photos from any of his company's rehearsals or events for literally two (2) full years. And, when photos were finally posted, I was the one who posted them, not him. Why not? Simply because he *still* hadn't learned how to edit his company's website.

How can you get people to support you and come to your online houses when you're not even active in them? It's like having a store that not only doesn't have any new products, but they also barely have any of the old products.

How many people do you think will come into that store? How many of the people who do come into that store do you think will come again or tell anyone else anything good about the store? Exactly. Only a few, if anyone at all.

7.) By him taking days off to do nothing productive, he was wasting valuable time which he could use to not only learn and master his business, but to also make headway on introducing his business to his potential customers in a timely manner.

8.) Now him traveling out of town for fun with his family almost every weekend is a little different because spending time with family is important. The problem was that he didn't understand the sacrifice that had to be made initially in order to breed entrepreneurial success (*That word 'initially' is the most important part of his story*). And part of that sacrifice would be time with his family, time fishing, time playing video games, time with his significant other, and more.

He should have had a talk with them and let them know that for the next few months he wouldn't be as available on a personal level because he needed to focus on getting the business up and running. However…

…instead of that, he tried to live the same lifestyle he did as an employee; one that garnered him much more time and a lot less responsibility. He wasn't willing to sacrifice for a small time in order to reap benefits for a lifetime.

To this day, that has been one of the biggest obstacles to the *consistent* success of his business.

9.) By taking people's word for it that they have an agreement on a business deal, and then stopping working on any other deals based off of their 'word,' he ended up wasting more time and missed out on other deals.

My friend is a trustworthy person, and one tends to project onto others who they are. If you're a thief, then you tend to think everyone is a thief. If you're a kind person, then you tend to give everyone the benefit of the doubt.

Chapter 10: 'Employer -vs.- Employee' Thinking.

He was getting verbal agreements from people that they were going to contract his company for their services, but I kept telling him verbal agreements only matter in court, and since he's not going to sue anyone about these 'agreements,' he needs to put his eggs in *written contract* baskets.

He didn't listen.

He repeatedly wasted time on waiting for people (*who verbally told him that they would contract his company*) to get back to him without going after other potential clients.

He'd talk to 10 people, three (3) would say they were going to contract his company, and then he would wait for two (2) weeks and hear nothing back from them, only to realize they weren't returning messages or phone calls because they'd discarded him.

He should have contacted 100 people. Then he might have gotten three (3) contracts swiftly. Instead, he got none and ended up having to go to the highest person in that industry in the city to get his initial deal.

10.) And one of the worst things that he did repeatedly was give himself an out for anything he didn't like, whether that out be someone else doing it or him giving repeated excuses for it just not getting done.

He was extraordinarily resistant to learning new things, so he didn't know a lot of the things that a business owner should know.

He would outsource literally every single possible piece of work that he could, and I don't mean outsourcing to outside companies. I mean outsourcing from himself to anyone else who would do it.

Unfortunately, by him doing that, he never learned how to do so many aspects of his own business. That meant that whenever someone, like me, wasn't available to do something, he could not get it done because he didn't know how to do it himself.

He ran into repeated problems because of this.

He missed deadlines, frustrated himself, and lost contracts because of not knowing how to do even the basic things that every business owner should know. That can be catastrophic to any business, especially a new one.

There was a saying that my parents said when I was a child that really stuck with me:

"Oh! You don't believe fat meat's greasy, huh?"

TRANSLATION: "You don't believe what I'm telling you? Well you'll find out soon enough."

I consistently repeated that saying to my friend over the years. One day, after yet again suffering the consequences for not listening to and applying what I'd told him, he sent me a meme of the Lion from the movie "The Wiz," and it had the Lion saying, *"I do believe fat meat is greasy!"*

****THE END****

Too funny, but also not funny.

On the way to his now budding success, my friend took unnecessary losses and ran into too many figurative brick walls. This was due almost entirely to him not wanting to let go of his employee mindset at the initial stages of his business.

Now, having been on the employee side of the fence as well, I can see why he wouldn't want to let that employee mindset go. That mindset put him in a much easier, more care-free lifestyle. Unfortunately, he learned the hard way that that mindset was a weight to his business' success.

In that previously-referenced viral video, the "Hip-Hop Preacher" also famously said:

> *"...when you get to the point where all you wanna do is be successful as bad as you wanna breathe, then you'll be successful."* ~ Eric Thomas

Truer words may never have been spoken.

REMEMBER: If you are in the employer position, but have an employee mindset and are not focused enough on your business to make it thrive, then, plain and simply put, it will not.

Chapter 11:

"Good Help Is Hard To Keep."

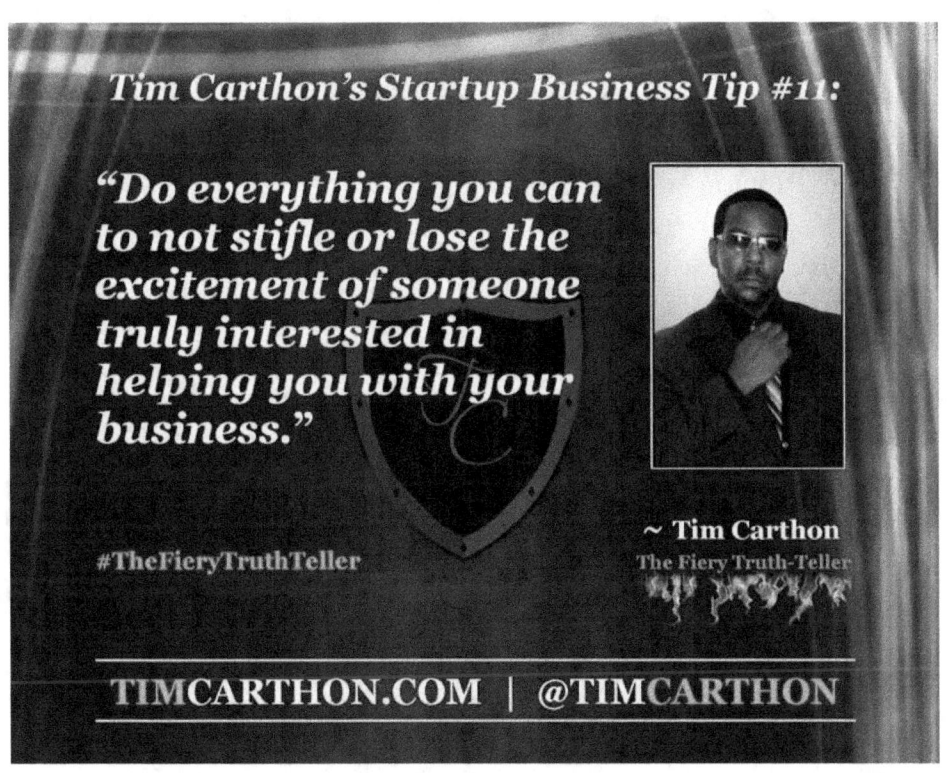

One thing that I've found in my entrepreneurial travels is that every single second that you waste can mean something detrimental to your business. The reason for that is because of something of which a clear example was shown to me again recently.

I was waiting on something important from a young lady who was volunteering for my business. I'd just had a major breakthrough mentally and, due to the type of breakthrough it was specifically, that also meant that I had a major breakthrough entrepreneurially.

I started working on an event and the young lady promised me that she would gather some much needed, major research for me. She initially told me that she would deliver the information on a Monday evening.

Monday evening came, but there was no delivery.

By Tuesday morning, the information still had not been received. I didn't sweat it because I knew that she'd had a long weekend with a number of church events, so I figured she'd fallen asleep. I asked her about it and she confirmed my initial thought and told me that she'd get the information to me by the evening.

By the next morning, there was still no information, so I texted her and asked about it. She, again, told me that she'd get the information to me by the evening.

Now I'm thinking that we're already halfway into the work week and I still don't have the information I was supposed to

Chapter 11: Good Help Is Hard To Keep.

receive Monday evening. However, I decided to wait and see if this would be the day where I finally got the info on which I'd been waiting.

Later that evening, about 6pm EST, I hadn't received any of the research. I told myself that she'd probably just gotten home from work and just needed a bit of time to get everything together to send, so I waited…

…and waited…

…and waited…

…and waited for hours, but I didn't receive anything. So, as usual, I texted her and asked about the research. However, this time, I didn't receive an answer from her. That was abnormal at this time, but, then again, she could have been sleep, so I decided I'd message her Thursday morning.

The next morning, I texted her about the information. I was hoping to get to her before she went to work, but I received no reply. I started to get the edges of this eerie, déjà vous feeling, but would wait to see if such a feeling was warranted.

All day I was waiting to hear from her, but I didn't receive a text, phone call, social media message, nothing. By the time the evening came, my déjà vous feeling had slipped from the edges to dead center in my mind. Was this volunteer about to leave without a proper goodbye? It wouldn't be the first time.

So, I started to prepare to not hear from them anymore. Tomorrow was going to be the day of finality. If I didn't hear anything from them, then I would consider them to have 'pulled an Elvis' on me.

Friday morning, I contacted them again about the research, but I only sent one short message:

> "Hello?"

And just like the past few days, I received no response. As the day went on, I was contemplating not just the seemingly inevitable leaving of the building by them, but the fact that this was the 5th day of me waiting on them to give me the information I needed. Now I know what you're thinking:

> "Why didn't you just get the information yourself?"

That makes all the sense in the world, until you find out that the information needed is so vast that I could not devote that amount of time to it. Why not? Simply because doing so would then delay and maybe even damage all of the work for my business that no one else but myself could do.

This is why it's so important to have a team that can work on different pieces of your business' puzzle *concurrently*.

So, when the evening came, I sent them another message about the research they were supposed to have gathered days ago and sent to me. The response I got was interesting. They told me that they were dealing with some personal issues and that I should "trust them."

Trust them?

Chapter 11: Good Help Is Hard To Keep.

I'd trusted that they were going to do what it was they said they were going to do initially, but what happened? They had not delivered what they promised when they promised. Worse yet, they hadn't even delivered anything at all other than broken promises. However...

...I could tell by the message they sent me that they were not in a good mental place. Their emotions were all over the place, and that's definitely not good for a conversation about any issues I may be having with them for information non-delivery, especially seeing as though they were volunteering and had absolutely no mandate to help me.

At that moment in time, I remembered how I'd previously lost the fire of an individual in an influential position who was helping me with one of my youth programs. They wanted to take my program national, but I wanted it to only be statewide at the most.

I didn't do anything wrong, but not doing anything wrong doesn't necessarily mean that what you did was correct. I remembered how her assistance fell way off after that; how her fire for helping me push the program completely died out, and it saddened me. I thought:

> *"Could I have done something different? Should I have done something different?"*

I told one of my brothers about this story, and he said something to me that solidified everything I was already thinking:

> *"You don't want to stop somebody who is helping you from helping you. If they want to help, just let them help."*

I will never forget that, for he was the first to put into verbal words everything I was already thinking.

Due to this, when it came to this young Lady who had not delivered the information I so desperately needed, I just decided to leave her alone after that Friday. No, not push her away from my business. Just leave her alone about it, at least for the time being.

The next day, I stopped sending her messages about what I needed business-wise and focused on what she needed emotionally.

From Saturday to the next Wednesday, any message I sent her had to do with how she was feeling and what was going on in her life. I had high hopes that she would one day surprise me. I'd joyously get an email notification with the subject line, "African-American Media Spreadsheet Info," or something to that effect, and I'd breathe a sigh of relief. However, by that next Wednesday night, I hadn't received a thing.

Something had to be done.

The next day, I sent her a message informing her that we needed to talk. Normally in relationships, be they business or personal, when a person says *"We need to talk,"* it's usually not good. This was no exception. It had been 10 days since she'd promised to get me the research I needed, but had yet to deliver it.

Time was literally being wasted because there were certain things that simply could not be done without that information, so I needed to put a halt to it. We agreed to talk that night, but her mounting circumstances kept her from keeping that appointment, so we ended up scheduling the conversation for the next day after she got off of work.

Friday evening, I called her. The first thing I did was explain to her how much I appreciated her help and that, if she didn't notice, I hadn't said anything to her about the information she promised me since last Friday.

I then began to tell her about how I stopped asking her about it because so many people who said they really wanted to make a difference in the world, and help me do it, seemed to fade anytime the slightest bit of pressure was perceived to have been put on them.

SIDE NOTE: I've never understood how one could be putting pressure on someone else (who actually agreed to do the thing which all of a sudden is causing pressure) simply by asking them to do what they said they would. Anyway…

I told her that she seemed to be on that path of fading and that she was too important to me to lose. At the time, it was a calculated risk. Do I risk losing her or do I hang on to her and risk doing damage to my business that might be irreparable?

I thought about the previous person who lost their fire for my business and I didn't want to lose another person who was truly excited about and interested in helping me reach my goals, so I checked the percentage of the two and came to a conclusion:

Losing the days was much less costly than losing her, so I should probably just stop asking her about the information; ceasing adding pressure to her already overcooked mental state, and just live to fight another business day.

And that's exactly what I did.

Turns out that was the best decision I could have made. She got me the information I needed by the next Tuesday and that information directly helped in landing me the biggest sponsor I'd ever had.

REMEMBER: You have to weigh options in business all the time. One thing that is always said is, "*Good help is hard to find.*" That is SO true. So, if you find someone who is great at what they do, but stumbles a little due to their humanity, don't be so quick to get rid of them or to do something that makes them leave.

Sometimes it's better to step back, reassess, and maybe take a smaller loss temporarily in order to gain much more for the greater good in the long-term.

Chapter 12:

"Where to Set Up Your Business Tents."

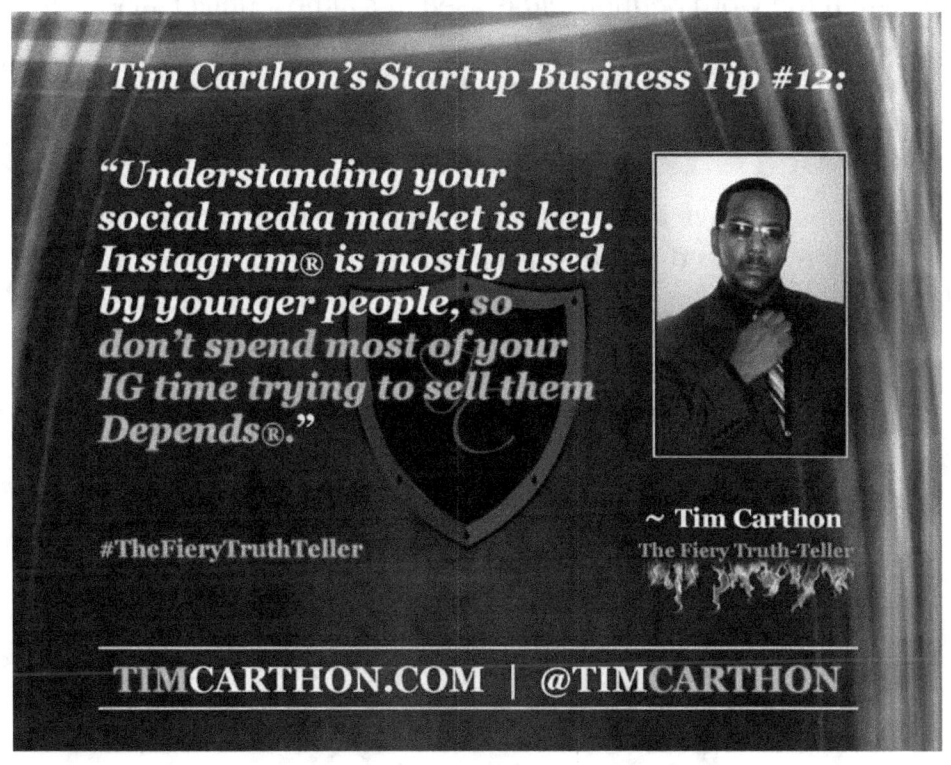

Have you ever gone somewhere and been there for a while, only to realize that probably wasn't the place for you to be?

You may have previously had a hint that something was wrong with where you were, but probably just brushed it off and rolled the dice, figuring you'd see what the future holds, only to realize finally that you wasted a ton of time and should have been gone from there a long time ago.

That's how it is in some relationships.

When the word *relationship* is used, it's almost universally regarded as something romantic, unless specific caveats are mentioned. In this instance, when I say the word "relationships," I don't mean romantically, at least not alone.

Yes, people have been in romantic relationships only to realize that they are in the relationship alone *emotionally*, which can be even more devastating. The late great comedian Robin Williams put it best:

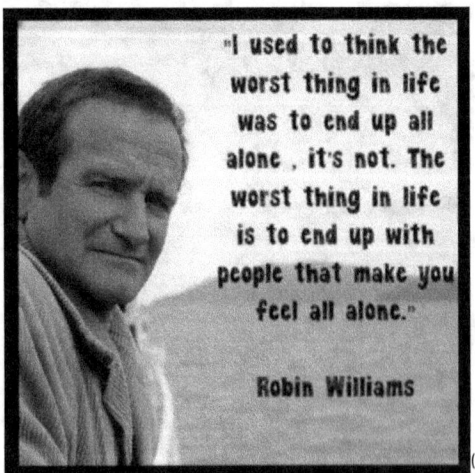

"I used to think the worst thing in life was to end up all alone , it's not. The worst thing in life is to end up with people that make you feel all alone."

Robin Williams

(17)

That definitely happens in romantic instances. However...

...the relationship of which I'm speaking is your relationship with your social media business accounts (*if you don't have any, you'd better get you some*).

Having a social media page on a site where you are doing everything you can to just get your family and friends to like/follow/subscribe is difficult. So, your company just being on *a* social media site is not as important as it being on *the right* social media site.

I started my social media experience on the social media site Facebook.com many years ago. I didn't really understand the depths and nuances of Facebook®, but, month after month, year after year, I posted and advertised my events, products, contests, and everything else of which I could think on there.

Needless to say, my work-to-reward ratio on Facebook® was abysmal.

All of these Facebook® "friends," 2,400+ of them. Family members galore. High school classmates. College colleagues. Yet, the only non-'Like my page' support I received for my business on Facebook® was when I spent hours upon hours daily directly begging people I knew through instant message to monetarily support one of my ventures.

It simply boggled my mind.

I just couldn't understand why I was not getting any traction from all of these Facebook® "friends," all the way up until two things happened:

1.) I realized that, in general, most people you know don't really care about your dream (*this subject should have a book all to itself Lol*).

2.) I started truly understanding the social media world.

The latter of those two happened when one day I actually posted to another social media site, Twitter.com, *directly*. Now I use the term directly because I *had* my Twitter® account linked with my business Facebook® account. This was so that every time I posted something to Facebook® it would automatically post to Twitter®.

I did that in order to save time. And, for a small business owner, saving that time of having to post to two different sites was invaluable, or so I thought.

So one day, after years of getting barely any support from individuals on Facebook®, I just so happened to decide to log into Twitter® directly and do a few posts, better known as "tweets."

I couldn't believe the response I received.

After 'favoriting' and 'liking' so many other *Tweeple's* posts (*yes, Tweeples = Twitter® people*), it was absolutely stunning. People started 'retweeting' things I did and liking and favoriting my tweets. Next thing I know, I started seeing notifications for "new followers."

Wait, what? What in the world was happening?

What was happening is that I was being rewarded for my interaction. I was being rewarded for my work. Needless to say, I felt more alive and supported on Twitter® in that one day than I had in all the previous years I'd been on Facebook®.

The question is, *why was this*? Not why did I feel more alive, but why was I getting support so fast on this social media medium that I had not been getting on the one I'd been using directly for so long? Once I did a bit of research, the answer was clear and made all the sense in the world.

I was on the wrong social media site for my business.

You see, social media sites are tailor-made for specific user experiences, or so they try to be. And be it age, race, nationality, sexual orientation, education level, career track, or other, those user experiences bring forth site users from all walks of life. These are all part of what's called *demographics*; statistical data relating to the population and particular groups within it.[18]

Currently, the top 10 social media sites and apps *worldwide* by users[19] are:

- Facebook® (*1.55B active users*)
- YouTube® (*1BM active users*)
- WhatsApp (*900M active users*)
- Tencent QQ (*860M active users*)
- Facebook® Messenger (*800M active users*)
- Qzone (*653M active users*)
- WeChat (*650M active users*)
- Tumblr (*555M active users*)
- Instagram® (*400M active users*)
- Twitter® (*320M active users*)

Here are the 10 top *American-used* social media sites by users:[20]

- Facebook® (*1.55M active users*)
- YouTube® (*1BM active users*)
- Tumblr® (*555M active users*)
- Twitter® (*320M active users*)
- Google®+ (*300M active users*)
- Instagram® (*400M active users*)
- Vine (*200M active users*)
- Reddit® (*174M active users*)
- LinkedIn® (*100M active users*)
- Pinterest® (*100M active users*)

So let's take a look at a few social media networks from a Business Insider® report based on age demographics data from Internet analytics company comScore®:

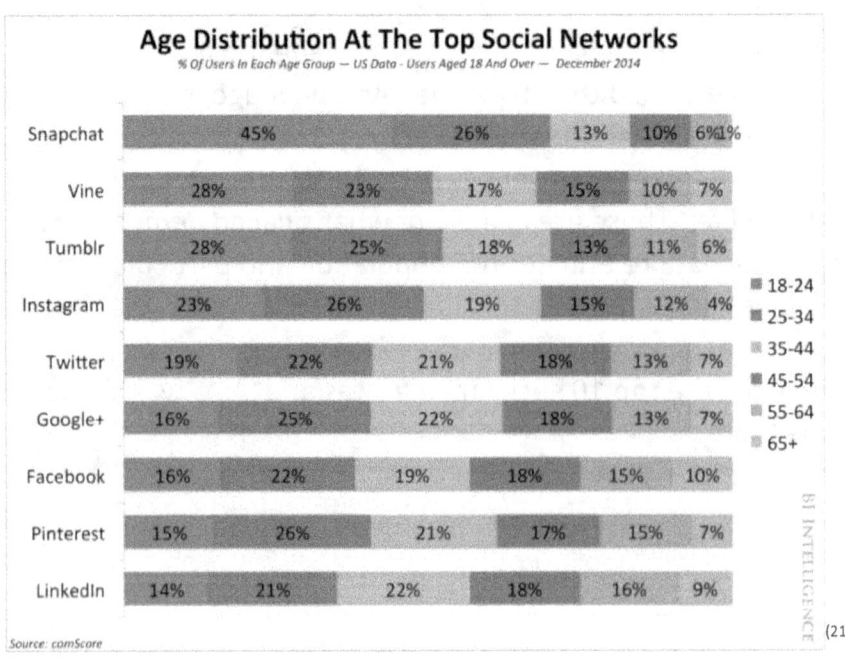

[21]

Chapter 12: Where to Set Up Your Business Tents.

For those of you who don't like graphs and charts, here's my generalized demographics translation (*that I tell my startup business infrastructure consulting clients*) of some of those social media sites based on the combination of my own studies:

- Snapchat® = Young adults and college Students.
- Facebook® = Family and friends.
- Twitter® = Entrepreneurs, newscasters, entertainment celebrities, and the die-hard fans who love them and the people *and trolls* who hate them.
- Instagram® = Teenagers and college Students, especially Greek-letter organization members.
- Pinterest® = Young mothers.
- LinkedIn® = 'Career-minded' business people.

So, by me being an entrepreneur, I realized that the reason behind the lack of support on Facebook® and the almost instant support on Twitter® was due to Twitter® being a better social media site than Facebook® for entrepreneurs such as myself to build our audiences.

Once that happened, it opened my eyes to every other social media medium, for what demographics they work best, and how to use them to build not just your audience, but your brand. Now I train aspiring entrepreneurs on the use of social media for their businesses.

REMEMBER: You want to have a presence everywhere, but you want to spend the majority of your business' *online time* on the social media mediums that will help build your brand the most. The rest will simply be an extension of that *one*.

Chapter 13:

"Fame, Fortune, And..."

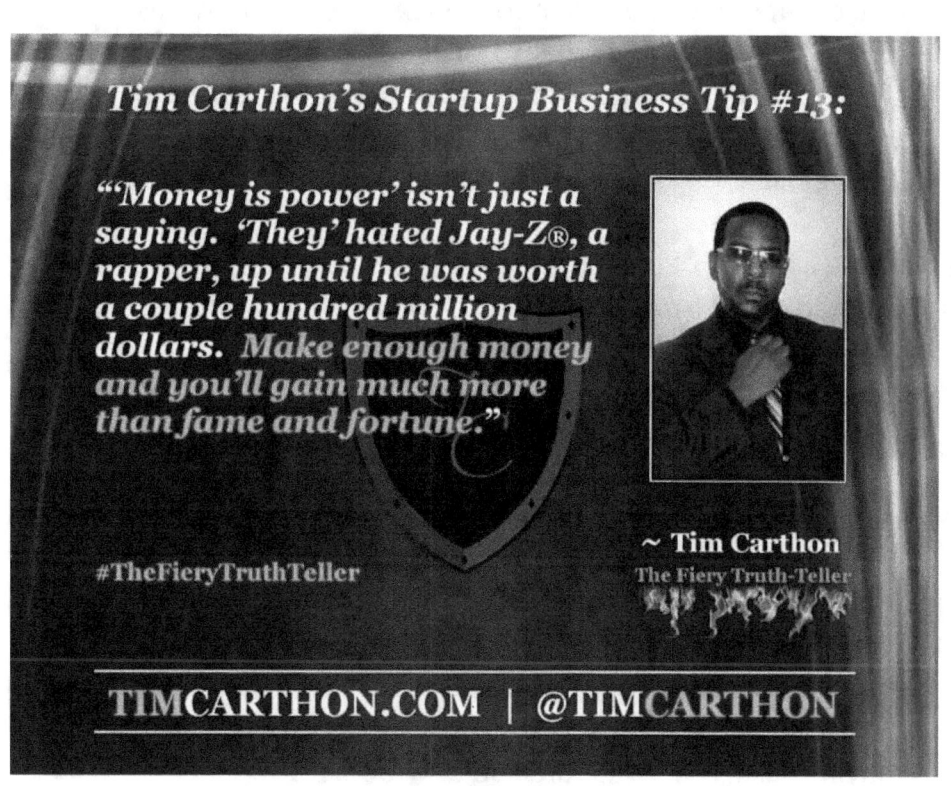

If there is one thing that I have learned about the world since I started into business, it's that *nobody cares about your dream*. Oh, you will have a few individuals who care about *you* and will try to help *you*, but they will more than likely not actually care about what it is you're trying to do. Not until this certain point in time:

When your company becomes successful and profitable.

Building a profitable business is more than difficult. It's rare. 90% of startups fail due to internal combustion, ranging from lack of capital to expanding too quickly, better known as 'premature scaling.'[22] That's not even counting how many of the remaining 10% *almost* fail. You have to take all of that into consideration before we can even begin to talk about actual profitability.

There are tens of millions of companies out there that are profitable and from which we buy products and services monthly and sometimes even daily. However…

…how many humans have there been in existence since the inception and the eventual profitability of all of those companies? Tens of billions?

Even if you said there were 500M profitable companies in the world since the beginning of the creation of the corporate business structure, what percentage is that of the amount of humans that have existed in that same timeframe? 3%? 5% maybe? Like I said, it's rare. So ask yourself:

What comes of that profit when it's made?

We know fortune comes, and, more than likely, that's followed by a certain lavish lifestyle. On top of that, certain levels of fame come as well, even if it's an individual or a company being only 'famous' within their business area of expertise.

So, what else comes with that profit?

Depending on the level of a company's profit, there are two powerful things that come along with that money:

Influence and control.

CONTROL

Now I talked about money and its influence previously in Chapter 8, but control with money is a more definitive thing than its predecessor.

Think of influence compared to control as *strong suggestion* vs. *mandatory*. Money currently rules the world, so, if you have money, it would beg to reason that you have some form of control of the world, or at least important people and/or things in it.

The funny thing about the power of money is that it can give you control of people and situations even if you don't actually use it. Oh, you can use the threat of it, but you don't *necessarily* have to spend the money itself.

Individuals who and entities that have large sums of capital can scare other individuals into doing their bidding just by leveraging what they *can* do with the "power of the purse."

Take any lawyer-based television series in history. What is one of the things that most, if not all of them, have said in their scripts at one time or another? Something to the effect of:

> "I'll have you tied up in court for so long that even if you win your grandkids won't see any of that money!"

TRANSLATION: *"We have so much money that we'll just stall for the next 10 years."*

And what usually happens on those shows after that type of threat? The threatened party folds and either cuts a deal or just lets the lawsuit go completely.

REMEMBER: When you're able to leverage your profits to where you can dictate the direct actions of others, that is a level of control that cannot be gained simply by having influence.

In other words, if you're not able to move something yourself, money can give you a level of control that can get you someone who or something that will move it for you. Just be sure to use that control for the *greater good*, not just your company's bottom line.

Chapter 14:

"The Art of Verbiage."

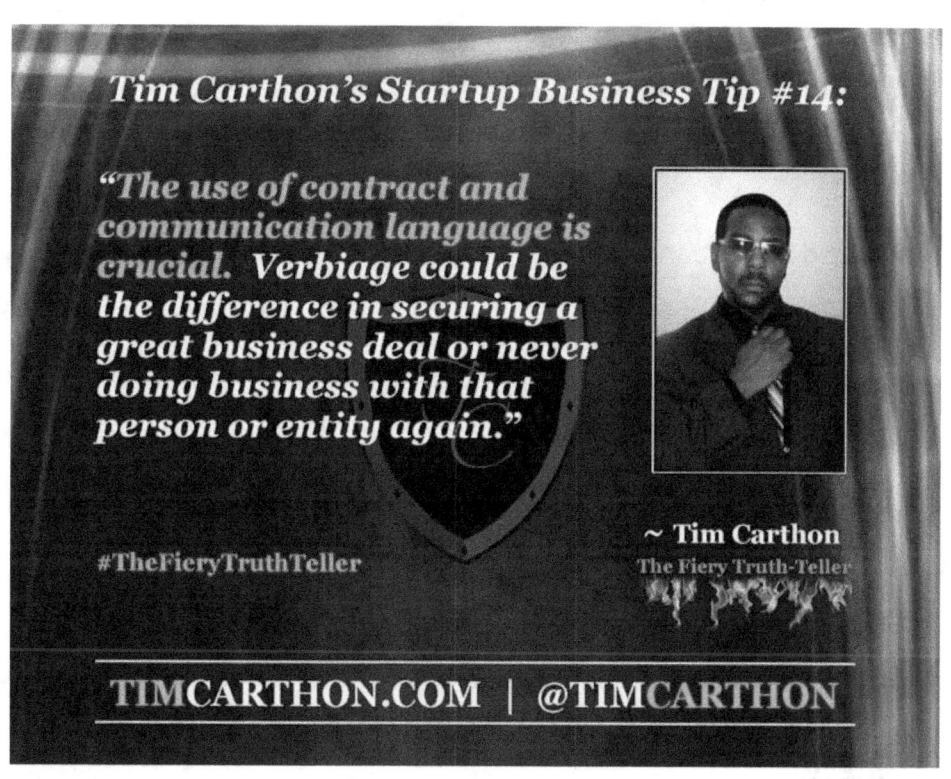

I have always been amazed at how people seem to not understand the power of their words. People get into arguments and say the most hurtful things purposefully, and, when the argument is over, they act like what they said wasn't *actually* said. Then when it's brought to their attention, they blow it off with the unoriginal dismissive statement:

> *"I was just mad at that time. You know I didn't mean that."*

Yes, you did mean *that*.

Words during an argument are like words from an inebriated person: Unfiltered, not un-meant. In business, your words have to be the exact opposite of the former, but the same as the latter.

Filtered and meant.

You transmit words in business through several mediums; verbal contracts, written contracts, emails, and traditional letters.

The verbiage you use in either of those is literally worth money; so much so to where the right or wrong verbiage can be the difference between profit and loss for your business.

CONTRACTUALLY

<u>**Verbal:**</u>

When a person or a company makes a verbal contract, via an authorized representative, that contract is supposed to be as iron clad as a written contract. However...

...proving that someone agreed to something specific verbally is difficult-to-impossible, especially if a person can come back later and state that the verbal agreement was never made due to lack of proof on your part.

In any case, when the agreement is made and both parties go to give what was agreed upon from their side, the agreement language that was used is of the utmost importance.

If you say, for example, "*I will give up-to 200 blankets...,*" that doesn't equate automatically to 200 blankets. That can be anywhere between 1-200 blankets. The words "up-to" are the most important words in that agreement because they negate specificity; giving the person making the statement a certain range of blankets that can be delivered instead of a definite amount of blankets required.

So be mindful of even your words when discussing possible agreements. You don't want to make a statement and end up inadvertently agreeing to something that will be detrimental to your business.

Written:

Written contracts are much more enforceable. Yes, there are several different interpretations of the meaning of words and phrases in context, but having a firm knowledge of the language with which you are writing the contract can help minimize both reasonable and unreasonable interpretations of its verbiage.

One of the most powerful, most used examples is the following phrase:

> "...but is not limited to..."

What that statement does is what lawyers call *"leaving the door open."* That simply means that whatever it is that precedes that statement is not the finale, if the person about whom it is speaking so chooses.

For example, me stating, *"My compensation is as follows:"* is one thing. Me stating, *"My compensation will be, but is not limited to, the following:"* is another.

The former gives a definite amount of compensation. The latter states part of the compensation, but 'leaves the door opened' for additional, unforeseen *potential* compensation (*i.e., bonuses, stock options, expense account*).

REMEMBER: Mastering the art of contract verbiage is essential to the protection and growth of you and your business.

WRITTEN CORRESPONDENCE

There are many different ways that we humans communicate; sound (*i.e., talking, mumbling, yelling, screaming, crying*), writing (*i.e., emails, letters, contracts, cards*), and body language/signals (*i.e., sign language, Morse code*). Although

Chapter 14: The Art of Verbiage.

the in-person touch is always the best, writing allows you to touch a much larger group of people in a much shorter period of time. And, as with any form of communication, there are rules.

Titles: One unspoken rule is that people like being referred to by their titles. It takes an extraordinary amount of work and sacrifice to get to certain points career-wise, and people want to be acknowledged for both that work and their sacrifice.

One way to acknowledge them is to address them by the title they've earned. Starting a letter with "Superintendent Jones" or "President Morris" is a sure way to at least get them to read the introductory paragraph.

Spelling and Punctuation Errors: Another rule (*that is actually a written one*) is that, when sending out your correspondence, you want to make sure that there are absolutely no spelling errors within it. Punctuation errors are bad as well, but at least with one of those your *might* be able to get away with it and not completely wreck their perception of you. However...

...spelling errors in business are a sign to people that you didn't care enough to 'prep their visual meal' *correctly*. It doesn't matter if you care enough. It only matters if they *think* you do, and grammatical erors are a sure way to make them think you don't.

Did you just catch that purposeful irony?

Yes, I spelled *errors* incorrectly. Now think about how you *just* felt when you saw that misspelled word *before* you knew it was purposeful. That's the risk in feeling that you take of the person reading your written correspondence every time you have spelling and punctuation errors within it.

So be sure to pay close attention to your spelling and punctuation when sending written correspondence. If you have to check it 10 times, walk away from it, come back to it, and then check it another five (5) times before sending it out, then do so. The extra due diligence will serve you well in the long run.

Same Sound, Different Meaning: Another check in the negative box is when you use one word that *sounds* the same, but the meaning is *not* the same. That is a turn off as well.

Take the *'their, there, and they're'* language assessment, for instance. Now *'their'* is a possessive pronoun. *'There'* is an adverb. And *'they're'* is a contraction meaning *'they are.'*[23]

You getting something as simple as this incorrect in your correspondence can simply irritate a potential client so much to where, from that moment on, that's all they think about whenever they receive a message from you.

Yes, that may sound a bit over the top and there may be a different way they could handle that, but you're trying to get their business, so they're entitled to feel any way they wish.

Email:

With the arrival of the digital revolution, sending messages to people has become fairly easy. One way to do so is through electronic mail, better known as *email*.

Unfortunately, email started being used not just for legitimate person-to-person, business-to-business, or person-to-business correspondence, but, just like the regular 'snail mail,' companies started using it to send out what was later dubbed "spam" (*unsolicited business emails*).

Unsolicited email advertisements got so ridiculous to where the government passed a law stating, in essence, that you cannot just send solicitation emails to anyone. They have to agree to be on your mailing list, meaning that they have to 'opt in.'

Spamming is an example of email abuse that can really turn someone off from your company. Fortunately, a lot of the spam from abusers who may not care about that has been curtailed due to them not wanting to be fined for breaking the *CAN-SPAM* law. However...

...there is one subtle way to turn potential customers off even when your email correspondence is in compliance with the law, you spell everything correctly, your punctuation is flawless, and your verbiage is masterful.

Over-emailing.

Emailing someone too many times within a short period of time can be extremely annoying and turn a potential customer completely off from not just the products and services you're trying to sell them, but from you as well.

You want to give people at least 3-5 days to respond to personal and business emails and at least 7 days in-between sending new 'general solicitation' emails (*i.e., newsletters, announcements*). Anything other than that breeds a higher risk of a negative response or no response at all.

Traditional Letters:

Traditional letters are a great way to show a client that you really care about them. There is nothing like the feel of paper in one's hands; a letter written on company letterhead, signed by one of the company executives, and stamped with the official company ink stamp or embosser. However...

...with traditional letters, formatting, just like verbiage and spelling, is also important. If you are a little rusty on the letter formats you were taught in school, be sure to check online to refresh yourself with the different formats in which a letter can be written (*I prefer block style*).

Now, a part of the formatting that a lot of people miss is the 'overwhelming' piece. You see, many times people try and fit everything they're thinking within a letter and the letter ends up being 2-3 pages long. Outside of it being a cease-and-desist order, a lawsuit, or inmate correspondence, it's a rarity that someone *fully* reads a letter that long.

Chapter 14: The Art of Verbiage.

The key is to write your letter in *novel* format; 2-3 sentences and then a new paragraph. If you use that as a barometer, then the eyes of the person reading that letter won't get tired just by initially seeing too much writing on the pages.

Even in writing this book, the tone used was thought about, mulled over again and again, and then decided upon. Once that was decided, the next phase came into play.

The verbiage had to match the tone intended. Chapters, words, and phrasing had to be checked and re-checked, and, even then, who knows if we will find a mistake somewhere within the covers 8 years from now? The point is...

REMEMBER: When writing, pay close attention to the tone, spelling, punctuation, and verbiage of what it is you're trying to convey and say, and make sure that it is as close as possible to everything that you wish to get across.

Chapter 15:

"Your Brand of Business."

Social media can be absolutely amazing. You can find childhood friends that you thought were lost forever. You can follow the lives of individuals you know as they get married, have children, buy a new car, a new house, and more. It's like an online reality show.

No, seriously. It's like an online reality show.

The level of drama that you can find on social media can be described in no less word than *epic*. As you can express yourself to multitudes of people with one click of a button, so can billions of others. And, in a flash, this amazing thing called social media can turn dangerous, especially for your business' bottom line.

Years ago when communication took a lot longer time to travel from one home to another, let alone one city to another, it was much more difficult for someone's reputation to be tarnished. Now, communication is transmitted in seconds from the street, the coffee shop, the car, the home, the office, the air, the beach, and virtually any place of which you can think, all with a mobile device.

That means that information about something happening overseas, which used to take months to communicate to just small portions of the world, can now be potentially communicated to nearly every aspect of the planet within literally seconds. That's a new level of power, and power such as this can be used subjectively for both good and evil.

Now imagine the CEO of a private Fortune 500® Company agreeing with and deciding to spout off on their social media

Chapter 15: Your Brand of Business.

account about a highly polarizing, unpopular opinion in their country. Imagine what might happen once people got wind of their 'rant?'

- There would be tons of people who like their post, but there would be many more who absolutely hate it.
- The comment section on that post would be filled with hatred, vitriol, and vague threats.
- People would start sharing that CEO's post on their own pages.
- A hashtag would be created specifically for that CEO (*#ThisCEOsAnIdiot*).
- Comments, shares, retweets, and reposts that include the '*#ThisCEOsAnIdiot*' hashtag would get so high to where the hashtag would start *trending* online within the country, and possibly worldwide.
- That trend would catch the eye of journalists looking for hot stories about which to write, especially seeing as though the person who is trending is an extremely wealthy and visible person.
- A petition boycotting the Fortune 500® Company would begin circling.
- Next thing you know, there would be a story on virtually every major news and industry website about how this CEO said something that got everyone in an uproar and got his company boycotted.

By the time the entire thing was over, that CEO would have issued an apology (*maybe even their resignation*) and the company would have taken a hit on revenue domestically and maybe even worldwide, all because of one post from a CEO that was massively unpopular.

This is the power of social media.

When it come to your business, it is important that you understand that, like becoming a member of a Greek-letter fraternity or sorority, once you're in it you become something 'additional' to others.

Take me, for example. I am a member of two (2) Greek-letter organizations. Due to this, in that world, I am no longer *just* Tim. I am Tim from KKPsi (*referring to Kappa Kappa Psi® N.H.B. Fraternity, Inc.*) or Tim the Alpha (*referring to Alpha Phi Alpha® Fraternity, Inc.*). People no longer see me as *just* me. They see me as myself *and* a representative of both of those fraternities.

Once you start a business, you are no longer *just* yourself. You represent more. You represent a brand. Your brand. And, on social media, you can make that brand something cherished or you can poke huge holes in it with your personal posts.

REMEMBER: People's perceptions feed their decisions and your choices feed their perceptions, so choose wisely.

Chapter 16:

"Time Flies."

Do you remember when you were younger and it seemed like you could play day after day for what seemed like forever, only to look up and realize that only four (4) hours had gone by?

And goodness, don't even get me started on the day before birthdays and holidays, especially Christmas. It seemed as though time jumped up off the clock and started running backwards just to slow itself down to a sadistic crawl.

Boy, those were the days.

Now you're older, and you're missing days:

> "Hey Jay, what's today?"
> "Wednesday."
> "Seriously? I thought it was Tuesday?"
> "No, B. It's Wednesday."

You're busier than ever, so time is evading you. As you're working, you hear the television in the background:

> TV: "Tonight on NBC® Nightly News..."
> You: "NBC® Nightly News? Wait, it's 6:30pm already? Dude, I just had lunch!"

You're swamped with much more important, time-sensitive work, so time is seemingly racing you purposefully:

- You have an 8pm deadline.
- You start working at noon.
- You look up one moment, it's 1pm.

- You look up (*in what seems like only a few minutes later*) and it's 2:46pm.
- Working frantically for what seemed like a little less than an hour, you look up and it's 5:03pm.

Time just seems to get more and more disrespectful of your need for it the older you get.

One thing that I've found to be absolutely bananas is how time seems to move extremely fast when you're working on your business. It moves even faster than it does when you are handling regular, everyday adult business, and this is why this chapter is so important.

Remember my friend in Chapter 10 whose business I helped start? Before then, I used to always try and talk with them about how they spent their money because they always seemed to have none, yet their bills weren't even half of what they made. After several years, they had a reckoning with the 'temporarily-unpalatable' truth.

One day, we were on the second floor of their parents' house. We were talking about money and, since budgeting is one of my specialties, I asked them to give me the ins-and-outs of their finances and bills, so they did.

I calculated approximately everything they made and on what they spent it the entire previous year. When I was done, I informed them that they'd wasted approximately $14,000 on things that they could no longer see.

Stunned, they refused to believe me.

So, looking over my written notes, I asked them, note for note, if the numbers were correct. They said yes. So I informed them again that they'd wasted $14,000 on pretty much nothing of long-term value.

They took my notes and just looked over them. I saw in their face the utter disbelief. Although an estimate, they were absolutely dazed at the direct-related news that $14,000 in expendable income had left their pockets the previous year, and they had absolutely no clue it had even occurred.

This *blind wasting of money* is all too common with people. And you'd probably not be surprised to know that it is the same way when it comes to people and their use of time as well.

We as humans tend to waste more time than we notice; seconds here, minutes there, all the while, like pennies in a jar, that time is adding up to hours, days, weeks, months, and even years over a lifetime.

When you are building a business, you cannot use time the way you used it when you were just living your regular, everyday life. Time moves differently…more swiftly. In essence, months become days while weeks become hours. You will look up at a deadline two months away and say to yourself, *"Omg, I don't have enough time!"*

REMEMBER: Use every moment you possibly can for your business. Yes, take time out for family and other things that help rejuvenate you and replenish the energy expended while working diligently on building your business, but do not *waste*

time. It has a funny way of showing you, in intensely hurtful ways, its lack of appreciation for your lack of appreciation.

Never forget this famous saying: *"Time waits for no man,"* and it waits for no business either.

Chapter 17:

"Survivors -vs.- Thrivers. Which One Are You?"

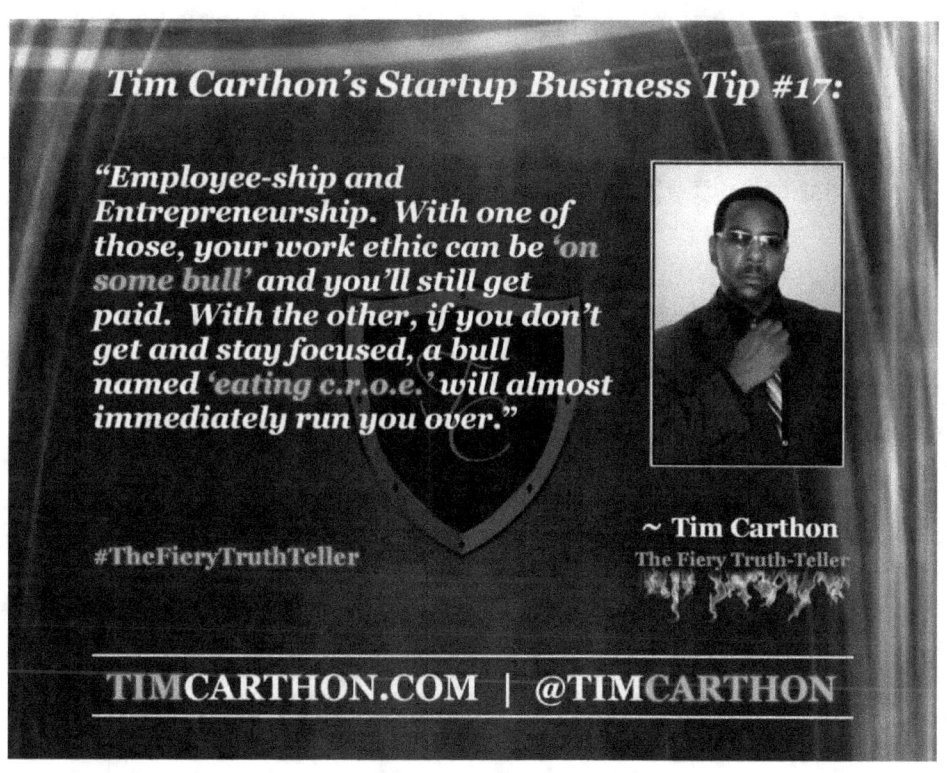

There was a social media post that showed an NBA® Player with several hundred Students, and the caption said, in essence, that they were sending 1,100 Students to college.

Now, on the surface that looks fantastic; them spending $41M to help provide higher education to all of those Students who finish the "I Promise Program"[24] (*yes, $41M out of their pocket*) and I truly applaud the amazing gesture. However, I felt a different way a little after I read the article attached to the post.

I was instantly reminded that the issue in communities around the country isn't having or not having a college degree as much as it is having an education and actual jobs available. What happens if you go to school for four years and come out during a statistically-low job placement period for college graduates?

Don't get me wrong. I love that they are giving back, but isn't the point of giving back to try and not just make *a* difference, but to make *the biggest* difference?

Who knows, the route this generous athlete took could turn out to be the biggest difference, not to mention that they can definitely do whatever they please with their money. However…

…since small businesses are said to create the most jobs (*due almost solely to an increase in their customer base's spending*), wouldn't investing half of that money in individuals starting small businesses, with a guarantee of 550 Students being sent to college being employed by those same small businesses when they get out of school, be a better plan?

Now I know what you're probably thinking:

> "But what if those businesses fail before the Students graduate?"

Simple.

Those Students would just do what they were planning to do if those businesses weren't even created: Attempt to get a job somewhere else with their college degree.

In any case, be they a life-long employee or a budding entrepreneur, either route for those Students would take massive amounts of work to become successful, which brings me to my next question:

Have you ever worked at a company that had an overly-lazy employee?

They think of their employment as a job instead of a career. These individuals care more about *staying afloat* than actually *getting out of the water* because floating in the same place is just A-Ok with them.

That type of worker, if you even wish to call them one, is a *survivor*, not a *thriver*.

SURVIVORS

The word *survivor* is usually used as a positive connotation, and rightfully so. It's generally defined as *"a person who survives, especially a person remaining alive after an event in which others have died...the remainder of a group of people or things...a person who copes well with difficulties in their life."*[25]

Not in this scenario.

See, survivors in this scenario are the types of goalless, visionless people who wish to do just enough to stay exactly where they are. Understand something: We're not talking about people who try hard, but seem sluggish all of the time or people who get tired quickly. We're talking about people who:

- Barely get their work done...
- Do the bare minimum needed to meet quotas...
- Turn in sub-par work at the last minute...
- Are always trying to find a reason to leave work early...
- Use every sick day as soon as they get it...
- Play way too much to where it consistently distracts others from finishing their work...
- (*Insert other time-wasting methods here*).

Ever wonder why they behave this way?

Outside of an actual mental disorder, they act this way in order to keep from having to take on any more responsibility. They're more of the *"At least I have something to eat"* than the *"I want something better to eat"* crowd. They have a titanium mental ceiling, and they're just fine with that.

At work, no one wants to be them and no one wants to follow them, yet these people can last at a company for decades simply because they ride the line of barely doing enough to stay employed. Unfortunately, they are usually the weakest links in a company and give the corporation no extra value.

Ever worked with an individual or individuals like that?

Whether you have or have not, be sure to understand that, if you are trying to improve things, these are individuals who you do *not* want on your team, especially the team of a company that you own.

THRIVERS

Thrivers are just the opposite of survivors. They are people who are looking to move forward in their lives and up in their careers. Thrivers are known to:

- Get their work done early…
- Go above and beyond to meet quotas…
- Turn in detailed, above-average-to-extraordinary work…
- Stay late because they're "zoned in" work-wise…
- Never take a sick day unless they're actually sick…
- Have fun, but they don't let fun take away from getting their work done properly and on time.

All of what they do is in pursuit of their *ladder-climbing agenda*. These individuals look to and usually become supervisors, managers, directors, vice-presidents, CEOs, and owners. They are the types of individuals you want on your team: *Self-motivated individuals*. They add immeasurable value to your company.

REMEMBER: As a business startup entrepreneur, every cent and every second matters when it comes to the survival and success of your company, and so does every team member. Build you a team of Thrivers and, like valuable chess pieces, set them strategically around you.

As famous and infamous business mogul Sean "P. Diddy" Combs once said, *"When building a team, you focus on the people who go hard for the team without you asking them to. Not the ones waiting on you."*[26] Just be sure that your team sees you going the hardest toward thriving than anyone else, because no one wants to follow a lazy leader.

Chapter 18:

"Fewer Employees, More Money."

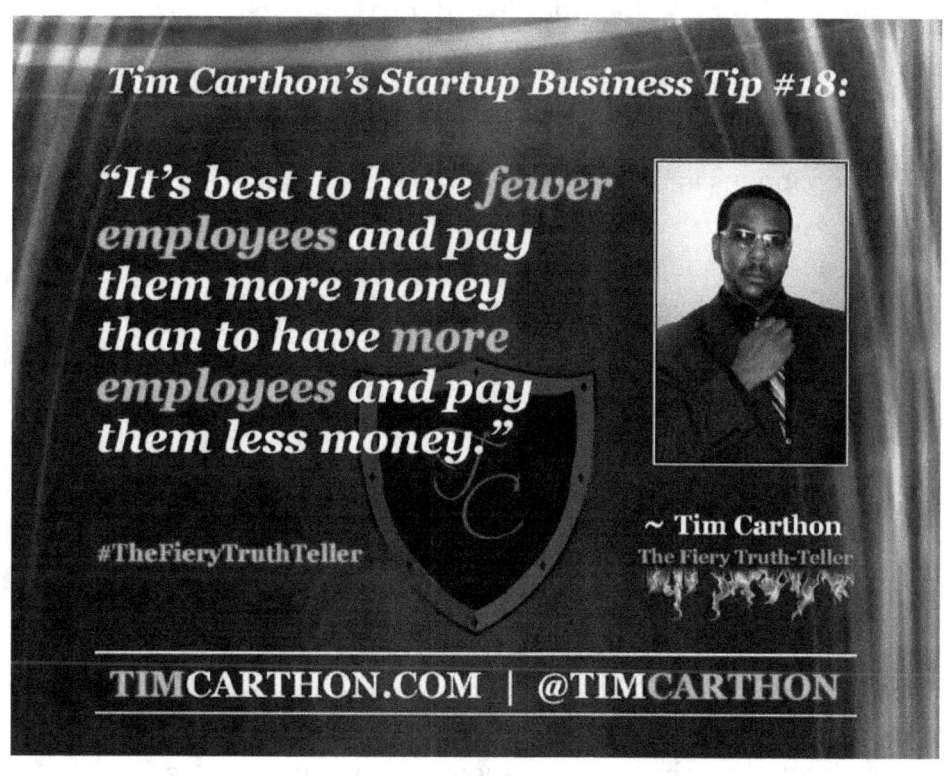

One of the biggest misnomers in business is that companies are job creators. That is not in any way true. Companies are job *place holders*. The job creators are actually the customers.

You see, when customers spend enough money at a business to where the business' inventory is being bought by them faster than inventory is being bought from the factories by the business, jobs are then created in the factories in order to keep up with demand.

Jobs are then also created in the stores that purchase the inventory from the factories in order to keep up with the amount of new customers coming in to purchase those products.

What happens in a recession is that economic activity slows down too much. When that happens, jobs can be lost because there aren't enough customers spending. The primary cause of this is not jobs lost. It's that more money is being saved by potential customers than spent.

See? No customers, no jobs.

The counterweight to this is to get potential customers to spend more money. The question as always is, how do we do that?

Ever heard the term *'expendable income?'* Expendable income is money that a person has attained that can be spent on absolutely anything without seemingly doing any negative damage to the lifestyle of the person spending it, be it temporary or long-term damage.

Chapter 18: Fewer Employees, More Money.

When you spend money that is *not* expendable, it gradually increases the chance of negative financial chain-reactions; chain-reactions which can permeate throughout the entire economic system of not only a person's personal finances, but their community's and eventually the country's as well.

So, expendable income is important and is what keeps the economy going in a positive direction growth-wise for extended periods of time. That begs the question:

How do we help people get expendable income?

As a business owner, one of the smartest things you could ever do is to pay your employees a higher wage than their actual position warrants. The reason for this is simple, economically viable, and wise.

Henry Ford, founder of Ford® Motor Company, famously said that he paid his workers the way he did so that they could afford to buy the cars that they actually helped make. There are several versions of his quote. However, two things about that are true:

1. In the years following his employees' pay increase (*double the previous amount he was paying them*), the financial move helped raised the profits of his company tremendously.

2. It made his employees much more loyal to him.

Profits + employee and customer loyalty? As an employer, is there anything better than that?

REMEMBER: When people have more money than they need, they will be more likely to buy things they want, all without doing damage to themselves or the economy. So, it's best to grow your company slower and pay your employees better in order to help spur the economy, which will, in turn, help create more jobs. That can do nothing but build a healthy, long-lasting economy.

Chapter 19:

"More Success Breeds More 'Support.'"

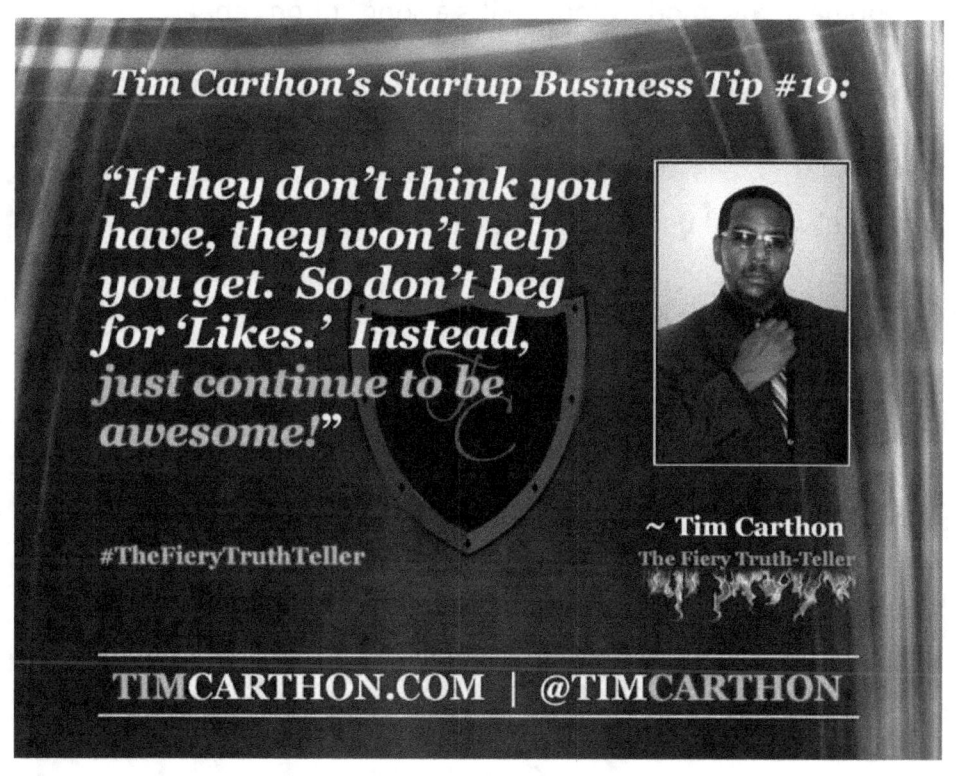

Although I have been in business for 14 years and counting, during my past six (6) years I had repeated visions of me being interviewed on Oprah Winfrey's television show on network television.

When she retired her show and went from someone else's television station to her *OWN*, pun intended, I then had visions of me being interviewed by her on her OWN network.

I never once thought about a multitude of questions that she would ask me. I only had one question that, to this day, keeps looping in my mind as though it's a song set on repeat:

> *"What is the most important thing that you've learned during all of your years in business?"*

My answer will be:

> *"That nobody cares about your dream."*

Now you're probably thinking that's a rather cynical statement, but I truly don't think it is. I know that saying "nobody" is definitely not true. That word will be purposely used to make a more piercing point.

You see, there have been people there to help me along the way. A few of those people cared about me and helped me because of me, not my dream. However, the others...well...it was a little different, to say the least.

One thing I've learned about people is that we love to shine. We love to be in the limelight, and anything that will help us to be seen, to shine, or to get some limelight is something for which we will somehow find some time.

During my business life, I found that the vast majority of the people who participated in my ventures weren't participating because they cared about me or what my dream means to me. They were participating because they felt *they* were going to get something out of it.

Think about this:

- When you buy a ticket to a concert, do you buy a ticket to someone's concert who you don't know personally or who isn't already famous?

Probably not.

When people buy concert tickets, they buy them for two (2) primary reasons:

1. For an artist who they know personally who may be on the rise.

2. For someone already famous.

Let's take buying a ticket to a concert for an artist who you know personally, be they famous or not. Now, although you're supporting them, let's be honest:

Did you really *primarily* buy that ticket to support them?

It seems like we do, but when you think about it, we probably only bought that ticket after the person we know started getting some 'buzz,' meaning that their name is starting to make its rounds through the city and/or music industry *artist-wise*.

That's the only way we can feel like we didn't waste our money on them. If we bought it when they looked like they weren't going anywhere, most of us would feel like we wasted our money. However…

…when they have buzz, it makes us feel good because we know them personally. We can tell people, "*Yeah, I went to high school with him,*" and we will get a few kudos for that. Hey, being next to a rocket that might fly into outer space can be exhilarating, right?

Now let's take buying a ticket for someone's concert who is already famous.

Are you buying that ticket to support them or to use their fame for your gain?

I'm fairly sure people do this one unconsciously, but I strongly believe it's the latter. People want to be a part of something great, so, instead of creating that greatness themselves, they will settle for being next to something and/or someone great.

This is why most concert tickets are bought, I believe.

Think of the most famous singer you know right now. Are they selling out concert venues because people want to support them, or because people want to be able to say:

Chapter 19: More Success Breeds More 'Support.'

> *"I went to the (*insert famous artist's name here) concert and I was only 7 rows back from the stage!"?*

It's like that on social media as well, but a little worse.

Although a click to share a post takes virtually no energy, people will almost only share things that will get them attention through "Likes" and "Comments" on their posts. It doesn't matter if what they shared is negative, vulgar, or graphic. If they think people will be interested enough for them to get attention, they will share it. However...

...if you're looking for them to share something dealing with your startup business or new music, that won't happen unless, again, they think you're on the rise to stardom. If that is the case, then you will get many more shares of and likes on your post. That is their way of showing you that they're with you, at least that's what most of them want you to think.

That is not the case.

People don't support others because they simply want to give. They support others because of what they get in return. Unfortunately, in the initial years of my current business, I had a bit of support that faded once they thought that my business wasn't going anywhere.

They didn't initially understand that the level of success after which I was going was rare and that it would take a Herculean effort both in time and resources to achieve. Once they realized the level of sustained work it would take, they didn't want any more parts of it. That was too much and too long for them.

This is when I realized that they didn't care about my dream. They only cared about what it was that my dream could do for them reputation-wise and potentially monetarily, and they wanted their shot of *microwave fame and money* right now.

Once I understood this, I stopped worrying about the masses *supporting me*.

I started spending my time on being great at what I do and building my business' brand, regardless of who was supporting me. Once I got really settled into that, I then took my time finding people *who cared about me* and were willing to go through the fires of time with me to reach the goals together.

That turned out to be less than 10 *non-family* members in 14 years.

So, it's me, its family, and my 10 'road dogs' 'till the wheels fall off, or until I become so famous that all of a sudden everyone wants to *help*.

REMEMBER: This is not about cynicism. It's about realism. It is decidedly important that we, as business owners, be intellectually honest and understand how our "supporters" think. In business, it's an exchange. It's the same way if they're paying or not paying for our products or services or even working for pay or volunteering.

They give us something, and we give them something in return. If they turn away because they think they're not getting something, make adjustments and keep it moving. Either they will come back because they looked again and this time saw that they could get something out of it again or they will find someone else from whom to get what they want. Be sure to never forget that.

Chapter 20:

"Issues -vs.- Problems."

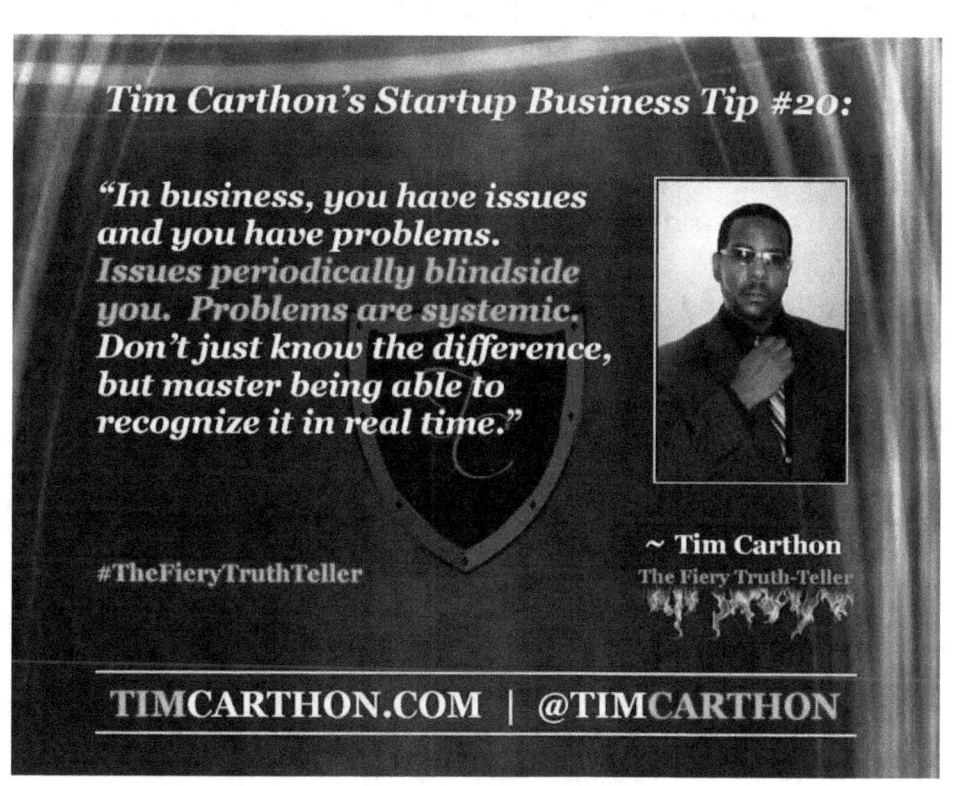

I want to tell you a story. And, as you may know, since there is a history of major tension due to racism and bigotry between 'law enforcement' officers and people of color in the United States of America,[27] I will use that as the mental backdrop.

Imagine a situation where police officers respond to a call for a domestic violence incident. The officers, while pulling up on the street on a side of town with which they are not at all familiar, are surveying the landscape to assess potential dangers and decide the best course of *initial* action.

Suddenly, they see a man exiting a house faster than what seems normal, and then he takes off running down the sidewalk in the direction away from them. The officers' training kicks in and it's immediately 'go time!'

The passenger-side officer swiftly exits the vehicle and calls for the man to stop, but the man keeps running. The driver cuts on the lights and the officers begin chasing the man down, one in the car and one on foot.

Within 10 seconds, the officer in the vehicle catches up to the man, slams on the brakes, jumps out of the car, charges at the man from the 7-o'clock angle, and nails him like a linebacker, tackling him to the grass in one of the neighbors' front yards and yelling:

> *"Didn't we tell you to stop, HUH?!"*, as he grabbed the man's hands and handcuffed them behind him, *"When we tell you to stop, YOU STOP!"*

Chapter 20: Issues -vs.- Problems.

By this time, the passenger-side officer had made it to the height of the scene. Little did either of them notice that the man wasn't responding, not until a bit of their adrenaline wore off. In fact, the man wasn't moving.

The officer stood up and then noticed something. He didn't see it before because of the color. It was green and they were on the grass.

It was a wire coming out of the man's ears.

They turned him over and followed the wire. Inside his jogging suit pouch was the man's phone with green earplugs attached to it.

They looked at the man's face and he was out cold. He'd hit his head on the ground from which the grass was growing when the officer tackled him.

By this time, a few residents had come out of their houses to see what the screech was they heard. It was the officers' car coming to a sudden halt. One of those residents was the individual on whose lawn the officers were currently standing and the man was lying.

As the officers called in the incident to the dispatcher, the residents watched as the man on the ground came to. The officers asked him if he was Ok. Once coherent, they stood him up and took him over to the police cruiser.

He asked the officers why they assaulted him and why he was handcuffed. They informed him of the domestic violence call they'd received and how, when they were pulling onto the street, they saw him come out of a house and start running.

Confused, the man explained to them that he was the only one in his home and was just going for his regular jog.

One officer asked him why he didn't stop when they commanded him to, and he explained that he had his earplugs in playing his workout music and didn't hear them telling him to stop. And, since they were behind him, he couldn't see them either.

Next thing he knew, he was waking up on the ground, handcuffed.

Overhearing the conversation, the residents confirmed the man's story, as his running was a daily occurrence in the neighborhood.

The man then asked if the officers had been given his address and the officers asked him what his address was. That question alone let the man know that the officers had not even checked to see if he'd even come out of the house that had the address they were given on it.

Infuriated, the man started verbally slaying the officers, not with volume but with wording. The neighbors joined in and started doing the same.

By the time the situation was over, the officers had apologized, missed the actual domestic violence perpetrator in the correct house, and angered the community even further. And you can imagine that a lawsuit was forthcoming.

This incident was an "issue," not a "problem."

These officers made a mistake in their assessment of and actions within a situation to which they were righteously called. Officers may be given an extraordinary amount of power within the country, but when it's all said and done they are still only human.

Now flip it.

Imagine those same two officers pulling into that neighborhood with no call specifically for them to be there. They're there because they have to reach their monthly quota for tickets and arrests. They pull up and see the exact same man do the exact same thing, and it's go time!

The entire situation plays out exactly the same, but this time the officers don't apologize at the end. They arrest and book the man for evading police and disobeying a lawful police order.

This incident is a 'problem,' not an 'issue.'

The issue in the first scenario was the bad decision making by the cops which was a mistake. That is something that can be easily rectified and may only be an issue with those two officers.

The problem with the second scenario was that the system itself set up catastrophic profiling and disenfranchising standards of police quotas for tickets and arrests.

This set the incentive for the two officers to make an arrest even when they weren't called to this side of town for anything in-particular, let alone a crime. It even incentivized doing it by any means necessary, even illegal and immoral ones (*racial profiling, making false arrests, filing false police reports, etc.*).

That is a serious problem and would take a massive overhauling of the entire law enforcement system to rectify.

You see, police officer issues are temporary, but law enforcement system problems are systemic.

In business, especially entrepreneurship, you have the same principles. There are parts of entrepreneurship that are irritating issues, such as not being able to find documents as quickly as you'd like for a particular fast-approaching deadline.

Yes, not being able to find that document is an issue, but that issue won't *necessarily* destroy your company in the short or long term. Why not? Simply because it could just be a blip on the entrepreneurial radar. However...

...if you can't find the document because the filing system for the company documents is discombobulated, then the so-called *issue* is actually a systemic *problem*.

Once realized, you have to move swiftly to rectify the problem or it could potentially eat away at your business until there is nothing left of your company but a shell of its former self.

REMEMBER: The key to successfully navigating both issues and problems is to think and plan long term. This will help in training you to recognize something that is just a temporary blip on your radar or a stealth bomber coming to take out your whole entrepreneurial dream.

REMEMBER:

"Your life was not given to you for you. It was given to you for you to be a blessing to someone else."

~ Tim Carthon

WORKS CITED

Chapter 1:

(wc.1) Mother Jones. *The Vulture Chart.* Digital image. *United States Senate.* Sen. Bernie Sanders, 01 May 2014. Web. 11 Apr. 2016. <http://www.sanders.senate.gov/newsroom/recent-business/the-vulture-chart>.

Chapter 3:

(wc.2) MarketWatch. *Netflix Inc.* MarketWatch, Inc. MarketWatch.com, 04 Oct. 2016. Web. 04 Oct. 2016. <http://www.marketwatch.com/investing/stock/nflx>.

Chapter 4:

(wc.3) Thomas, Eric. "When You Want to Be Successful as Bad as You Want to Breathe..." Eric Thomas Homepage. ETInspires.com, 07 July 2015. Web. 16 Apr. 2016. <http://ETInspires.com>.

(wc.4) Nick Ens. (TruWarior8). "Floyd Mayweather: Success. How Bad Do You Want It?" YouTube®. YouTube.com, 25 Sept. 2011. Web. 16 Apr. 2016. <https://www.youtube.com/watch?v=7SjbHJ28iec>.

Chapter 6:

(wc.5) Dredge, Stuart. "MySpace – what went wrong: 'The site was a massive spaghetti-ball mess'." Guardian News and Media Ltd. TheGuardian.com, 06 Mar. 2015. Web. 12 Apr. 2016. <https://www.theguardian.com/technology/2015/mar/06/myspace-what-went-wrong-sean-percival-spotify>.

(wc.6) Protalinski, Emil. "Facebook passes 1.55B monthly active users and 1.01B daily active users." Venture Beat. VentureBeat.com, 04 Nov. 2015. Web. 12 Apr. 2016. <http://venturebeat.com/2015/11/04/facebook-passes-1-55b-monthly-active-users-and-1-01-billion-daily-active-users>.

(wc.7) Facebook®. "Investor Relations" Facebook®, Inc. Investor.FB.com, 27 Jan. 2016. Web. 12 Apr. 2016. <http://investor.fb.com/releasedetail.cfm?ReleaseID=952040>.

(wc.8) Froelings, Lisa. "MySpace Sold – Again" Small Business Trends LLC. SmallBizTrends.com, 18 Feb. 2016. Web. 12 Apr. 2016. <http://smallbiztrends.com/2016/02/myspace-sold-again.html>.

(wc.9) Spangler, Todd. "Time Inc. Buys MySpace Parent Company Viant." Variety Media, LLC. Variety.com, 11 Feb. 2016. Web. 12 Apr. 2016. <http://variety.com/2016/digital/news/time-inc-myspace-viant-1201703860>.

Chapter 7:

(wc.10) Google®. *Conglomerate Definition.* Google®, Inc. Google.com, N.d. Web. 12 Apr. 2016. <https://www.google.com/webhp?sourceid=chrome-instant&rlz=1C1TSNP_enUS576US576&ion=1&espv=2&ie=UTF-8#q=conglomerate%20definition>.

(wc.11) PepsiCo®. "*Top Global Brands.*" PepsiCo®. PepsiCo.com, N.d. Web. 12 Apr. 2016. <http://www.pepsico.com/brands>.

Chapter 8:

(wc.12) Cornel University Law School. "Fiduciary Duty." Cornel University. Cornell.edu, N.d. Web. 15 Apr. 2016. <https://www.law.cornell.edu/wex/fiduciary_duty>.

(wc.13) Stitt, Robert. "You won't believe how much money Michael Jackson gave to charity." FinancialJuneteenth. FinancialJuneteenth.com, 30 June 2015. Web. 15 Apr. 2016. <http://financialjuneteenth.com/you-wont-believe-how-much-money-michael-jackson-gave-to-charity>.

(wc.14) The Recording Academy®. "Beyonce Past Grammy Awards." The Recording Academy®. Grammy.com, N.d. Web. 15 Apr. 2016. <http://www.grammy.com/artist/beyonce>.

(wc.15) Gerencer, Tom. "Beyonce Net Worth." Money Nation. MoneyNation.com, 04 Mar. 2016. Web. 15 Apr. 2016. <http://moneynation.com/beyonce-net-worth>.

(wc.16) Look To The Stars. "Beyonce Charity Work, Events and Causes" Look To The Stars. LookToTheStars.org, N.d. Web. 15 Apr. 2016. <https://www.looktothestars.org/celebrity/beyonce>.

Chapter 12:

(wc.17) Robin Williams. Digital image. "The Death of Celebrity & the Questions of Our Own Mortality." And The Geek Shall (Inherit the Earth). Wordpress.com, Web log. 08 Dec. 2014. Web. 16 Apr. 2016. <https://andthegeekshall.wordpress.com/tag/rip-robin-williams>.

(wc.18) Google®. "Demographics Definition." Google®, Inc. Google.com, N.d. Web. 15 Apr. 2016. <https://www.google.com/webhp?sourceid=chrome-instant&ion=1&espv=2&ie=UTF-8#q=demographics%20definition>.

(wc.19) Statistica. "Leading social networks worldwide as of January 2016, ranked by number of active users." The Statistics Portal. Statistica.com, N.d. Web. 14 Apr. 2016. <http://www.statista.com/statistics/272014/global-social-networks-ranked-by-number-of-users>.

(wc.20) Sareah, Faiza. "Interesting Statistics for the Top 10 Social Media Sites." Small Business Trends LLC. SmallBizTrends.com, 26 July 2015. Web. 14 Apr. 2016. <http://smallbiztrends.com/2015/07/social-media-sites-statistics.html>.

(wc.20) Kapko, Matt. "15 social networks with the most active users in 2015." CXO Media Inc. CIO.com, 11 Dec. 2015. Web. 14 Apr. 2016. <http://www.cio.com/article/3014362/social-networking/15-social-networks-with-the-most-active-users-in-2015.html#slide6>.

(wc.20) Statistica. "Number of unique U.S. visitors to Flickr from January 2012 to July 2015." The Statistics Portal. Statistica.com, N.d. Web. 14 Apr. 2016. <http://www.statista.com/statistics/252566/number-of-unique-us-visitors-to-flickrcom>.

(wc.20) The Social Media Hat. "Social Media Active Users 2016." The Social Media Hat. TheSocialMediaHat.com, 01 Apr. 2016. Web. 14 Apr. 2016.

<https://www.thesocialmediahat.com/active-users>.

(wc.21) comScore® and BI Intelligence. Digital Image. "UPDATE: A Breakdown of the Demographics for Each of the Different Social Networks." Business Insider, Inc. BusinessInsider.com, 29 June 2015. Web. 14 Apr. 2016. <http://www.businessinsider.com/update-a-breakdown-of-the-demographics-for-each-of-the-different-social-networks-2015-6>.

Chapter 13:

(wc.22) UC Berkey and Stanford University. *Startup Genome Report Extra on Premature Scaling (2012)*: 4. Amazon Web Services. AmazonAWS.com, Mar. 2012. Web. 12 Apr. 2016. <https://s3.amazonaws.com/startupcompass-public/StartupGenomeReport2_Why_Startups_Fail_v2.pdf>.

Chapter 14:

(wc.23) English Plus. "Their, There, or They're?" ~ English Plus. EnglishPlus.com, N.d. Web. 12 Apr. 2016.
<http://EnglishPlus.com/grammar/00000256.htm>.

Chapter 17:

(wc.24) Associated Press®. "LeBron's foundation to spend $41M to send kids to college" AP. FoxSports.com, 13 Aug. 2015. Web. 12 Apr. 2016. <http://www.foxsports.com/nba/story/lebron-james-college-scholarships-akron-university-cavaliers-i-promise-081315>.

(wc.25) Google®. "Definition of Survivor." Google®, Inc. Google.com., N.d. Web. 12 Apr. 2016. <https://www.google.com/webhp?sourceid=chrome-instant&ion=1&espv=2&ie=UTF-8#q=definition%20of%20survivor>.

(wc.26) Diaz, Hanna. "Puff Daddy Quotes Motivation." QuotesGram. QuotesGram.com, N.d. Web. 12 Apr. 2016.
<http://quotesgram.com/puff-daddy-quotes-motivation/#kszUdMlykt>.

Chapter 20:

(wc.27) Kappeler, Ph.D., Victor E. "A Brief History of Slavery and the Origins of American Policing." Eastern Kentucky University. EKU.edu, 07 Jan. 2014. Web. 12 Apr. 2016.
<http://plsonline.eku.edu/insidelook/brief-history-slavery-and-origins-american-policing>.

ABOUT THE AUTHOR

Known as 'The Fiery Truth-Teller,' Tim Carthon is a specialist in startup business infrastructure, a long time at-risk youth advocate, keynote speaker, author, and educator, and a proud father of his namesake TJ. Mixed with his passion for telling the "fiery truth" and helping people, he is using his extensive knowledge of and perspective on startup business infrastructure to 'uniquely' assist individuals in inner cities in removing fear and doubt and following their business ownership dreams. Tim accomplishes this through his exclusive E2 Seminar (*Economic Enlightenment Seminar*) and SBI Workshop™ (*Startup Business Infrastructure Workshop*™). His saying and life's motto: "*Your life was not given to you for you. It was given to you for you to be a blessing to someone else.*"

Website:
www.TimCarthon.com

Social Media:
@TimCarthon

www.ingramcontent.com/pod-product-compliance
Lightning Source LLC
Chambersburg PA
CBHW071817200526
45169CB00018B/354